EASY ITALIAN COOKING
Luciana Bianchi

EASY ITALIAN COOKING

Luciana Bianchi

Larousse & Co., Inc., New York

© Ward Lock Limited 1982
Illustrations © Orbis-Verlag für Publizistik 1982

First published in the United
States by Larousse & Co., Inc.,
572 Fifth Avenue, New York, N.Y. 10036

ISBN 0-88332-328-1
Library of Congress No. 83-82234

All rights reserved.

Printed and bound in Hong Kong by
Lee Fung Asco Ltd.

Notes

All spoon measures are level.

Each dish will serve four people, unless indicated otherwise.

Flour is all purpose and sugar is granulated, unless indicated otherwise.

Olive oil is plentiful and relatively inexpensive in Italy, where it is used generously in many dishes. Other vegetable oils may be substituted, but olive oil must be used if an authentic flavor is to be obtained.

CONTENTS

Appetizers and Soups 6

Pasta, Rice and Pizza 14

Fish and Shellfish 32

Meat and Poultry 38

Vegetables and Salads 56

Sauces 70

Desserts, Cakes and Pastries 73

Index 80

APPETIZERS AND SOUPS

Florentine Oysters

1 lb. spinach, washed, picked over and chopped
2 tbs. butter
salt, grated nutmeg
24 oysters, shelled (see below)
½ cup grated Parmesan or Emmenthal cheese
4 tbs. butter, melted

SAUCE
4 tbs. butter
¼ cup flour
1 pint warm milk
salt, pepper
1 egg yolk
2 tablespoons light cream
¼ cup grated Parmesan cheese

To make the sauce, melt the butter in a pan, stir in the flour and cook for 2 minutes without browning. Add the milk, bring to the boil, stirring, and cook for a further 2 minutes. Season with salt and pepper and remove from the heat. Whisk the egg yolk, cream and cheese together, stir in a little of the warm sauce, add to the rest of the sauce and keep warm.

Sauté the spinach in the butter for 5 minutes. Season with salt and nutmeg. Divide between four ovenproof dishes. Add 6 oysters to each dish and cover with the cheese sauce. Scatter grated cheese over the top and trickle melted butter over. Brown in the oven 425°.

The correct way to open oysters with an oyster knife: Hold the oyster firmly, with a dish towel over your hand. Apply the knife to the side of the shell, inserting it at the hinge to break the shell open.

Antipasti

Antipasti are the Italian version of *hors d'oeuvres*. An excellent opportunity to use your imagination in preparing small, piquant delicacies. It is impossible to give precise quantities, your best course is to assemble a dish of *antipasti* from whatever you happen to have in the refrigerator. Here are some suggestions:

Roll up slices of mortadella and stuff with capers. Add coiled-up anchovies and slices of hard-boiled egg.
Fill artichoke bottoms with Béarnaise sauce. Add a few black olives and some salad.
Garnish slices of smoked salmon with cress. Add a lemon slice garnished with caviar or lumpfish roe and some stuffed green olives.
Wrap chilled pieces of melon in smoked ham. Add slices of celery and carrot slices cut into a decorative shape with a serrated knife, dressed with a little oil, vinegar, salt and pepper.
Season tomato quarters with salt and pepper, place onion rings on top, garnish with cocktail onions, add a little oil and vinegar.
Dress asparagus with oil, vinegar, salt and pepper; garnish with chopped hard-boiled egg.
Arrange canned tuna fish with artichoke hearts in salad dressing. Garnish with strips of red pepper and celery leaves.
Serve *antipasti* with rolls and butter.

Antipasti

Calzoni

¼ oz fresh yeast or 1 teaspoon dried yeast
sugar
about ½ cup lukewarm water
2 cups flour
½ teaspoon salt
1 egg yolk, beaten

FILLING
1–2 tablespoons olive oil
½ cup ham, diced
4 oz mushrooms, chopped
1 onion, finely chopped
1 clove garlic, finely chopped
1 tablespoon chopped parsley
6 oz mozzarella cheese
3 oz salami, sliced
salt, pepper
1 teaspoon dried basil
1 egg yolk

To make the dough, mix the fresh yeast with a pinch of sugar and a little of the water, then add the remaining water. (If using dried yeast, dissolve ¼ teaspoon sugar in the water, sprinkle on the yeast and stir well.) Leave to stand in a warm place for about 10 minutes. Meanwhile sift the flour and salt into a bowl. Make a hollow in the centre and pour in the yeast mixture. Fold the flour over the yeast and mix, adding more water if necessary. Turn on to a lightly floured surface and knead for 10 minutes until you have a smooth dough. Return to the bowl, cover and leave in a warm place for about 1 hour until double in size.

To make the filling, heat the oil in a pan and fry the ham for 2 minutes. Add the mushrooms, onion and garlic and cook for 5 minutes longer. Stir in the parsley. Cut the cheese and salami into thin strips and mix into the ham and mushroom mixture. Season to taste with salt, pepper and basil. Take the pan off the heat and bind the mixture with the egg yolk.

Roll out the dough very thinly on a lightly floured surface. Cut out circles 4½ inches in diameter. Put some of the filling on half of each circle. Brush the edges with water, fold the circles in half, sealing in the stuffing. Brush with beaten egg yolk and place on a greased baking sheet. Bake at 450° for 20 minutes.

Calzoni

Salami Bolognese-style

Salami Bolognese-style

2½ cups stock
1 teaspoon wine vinegar
1 tablespoon white wine
sugar
1 envelope gelatine
1 egg white, lightly beaten
7 oz cream cheese
1 tablespoon sour cream
¼ cup grated Parmesan cheese
4 oz mixed pickles, finely
  chopped
12 large slices salami
about 4 tablespoons
  mayonnaise
2 teaspoons chopped parsley
sprigs parsley

Season the cold stock to taste with vinegar, wine and sugar. Melt the gelatine in a little of the stock over a pan of hot water. Add to the stock and stir well. To clear the jelly, add the egg white. Bring the stock nearly to the boil, skimming several times. Remove from the heat, cover and leave for 15 to 20 minutes, until the contents are perfectly clear. Strain through a piece of damp cheesecloth. Strain again if the liquid is still quite clear. Leave to cool in the refrigerator. As the jelly is begininning to set, turn it into a large oiled dish. Return it to the refrigerator and leave it to finish setting.

Mix the cream cheese with the sour cream. Mix in the grated cheese and chopped pickles. Spread this mixture on the slices of salami, bring two sides of the salami together to enclose the stuffing and fasten with toothpicks. Dice the aspic jelly and arrange on a dish. Place the salami rolls on top of the aspic. Decorate the rolls with mayonnaise and sprinkle with chopped parsley. Garnish the dish with parsley sprigs.

Fonduta

SERVES 5

1 cup milk
4 cups coarsely grated fontina,
  Emmenthal or gruyère cheese
salt, pepper
4 eggs
1 cup dry white wine
1 oz canned white truffles
1 small French loaf, diced

This is one of the best of all cheese fondue dishes. The truffles are not cheap, but they make a great deal of difference.

Heat the milk in a pan, add the cheese and beat well together. Pour into the fondue pan. Heat, stirring constantly, then add seasoning. Cook gently for 5 minutes, stirring constantly. Whisk the eggs with the wine, then add to the fondue pan, stirring hard. You want a smooth, thick, creamy mixture.

Cut the truffles into very small dice and add to the fondue. Place the fondue dish over its heater. Each guest spears a piece of bread on his fondue fork and dips it into the cheese mixture.

Florentine minestrone

Pancakes in Broth

¾ cup flour
salt, pepper
1 egg
2 egg yolks
¼ cup milk
½ cup water
oil for frying
½ cup grated Parmesan cheese
4 cups stock
1 tablespoon chopped parsley

To make the pancake batter, sift the flour and salt into a bowl. Make a well in the centre. Beat the egg and egg yolks and add them to the bowl. Mix slowly to a smooth batter, adding the milk and water gradually. Allow to stand for 30 minutes.

Heat the oil in a small pan and make eight very thin pancakes, one after the other. As each one is taken out of the pan, sprinkle with grated cheese and roll up. Place the pancakes in a hot soup tureen. Heat the stock, season to taste and pour over the pancakes. Sprinkle with parsley and serve.

Florentine Minestrone

2 tablespoons olive oil
¼ cup bacon, diced
2 onions, chopped
2 leeks, sliced
¾ lb carrots, diced
1 lb turnips, diced
¼ celeriac root (optional), diced
¾ lb Savoy cabbage, thinly sliced
1 small potato, diced
1 lb tomatoes, skinned, seeded and chopped
6 cups stock
salt, pepper
½ clove garlic
¼ cup macaroni
¼ cup rice, washed and drained
1 tablespoon chopped parsley
¼ cup grated Parmesan cheese

Heat the oil in a soup pan and fry the bacon gently for 2 minutes. Add the prepared vegetables except for the potato and tomatoes. Fry all together, stirring, for 5 minutes. Add the stock and seasoning. Mince the garlic with salt. Add to the soup. Cook over a medium heat for 20 minutes. Meanwhile cook the macaroni in plenty of boiling salted water for 10 minutes, drain.

Add the rice and diced potato to the soup. Cook for a further 15 minutes, then add the tomatoes and macaroni and cook for 5 minutes more or until the rice is tender. Sprinkle with parsley, and serve the grated cheese separately.

Neapolitan beef soup

Neapolitan Beef Soup

½ lb beef marrowbones
6 cups water
½ lb brisket
1 onion, chopped
1 stick celery, chopped
1 carrot, chopped
1 leek, chopped
salt
2 peppercorns
1 clove
½ bay leaf
2 juniper berries
1 cup macaroni
1 cup cooked ham
½ celeriac root
2 tablespoons concentrated tomato paste
2 teaspoons chopped chervil
OR 1 teaspoon dried chervil
¼ cup grated Parmesan cheese

Put the marrowbones and water in a soup pan and bring to the boil. Skim and simmer for 5 minutes. Add the beef, onion, mixed vegetables, salt, peppercorns, clove, bay leaf and juniper berries. Cover and simmer gently for 1 hour 20 minutes, skimming occasionally. Take out the meat and pass the soup through a fine sieve. Remove any fat if necessary. Return the soup to the pan.

Cook the macaroni in plenty of boiling salted water for about 15 minutes until tender. Drain. Meanwhile, remove any fat from the ham and the cooked beef. Cut the ham into strips about 1 inch long and ½ inch wide, and the beef into ¾ inch cubes. Slice the celeriac into small, thin strips. Dilute the tomato paste with a little of the soup and stir into the pan. Add the ham, beef, celeriac and macaroni and reheat the soup. Sprinkle with chervil and serve the grated cheese separately.

Roman soup

Roman Soup

3 tbs butter
¼ cup bacon, diced
1 onion, chopped
1 clove garlic, chopped
1 stick celery, chopped
1 carrot, chopped
1 leek, chopped
4 cups stock
¼ cup shell pasta
1 cup cooked ham
1 tablespoon chopped parsley
½ cup grated Parmesan cheese

Heat the butter in a soup pan and fry the bacon gently for 2 minutes. Add the onion, garlic and mixed vegetables, and fry for 5 minutes. Add the stock. Bring to the boil, cover and cook over a medium heat for 10 minutes. Add the pasta and cook for a further 10 minutes. Cut the ham into narrow strips ¾ inch long and add to the soup. Scatter the parsley on top and serve the grated cheese separately.

Fish soup

Fish Soup

4 medium tomatoes, skinned, halved and seeded
½ cup water
1 onion, chopped
1 clove garlic, crushed
salt
1 bay leaf
¼ teaspoon dried marjoram
1 teaspoon grated lemon rind
4 peppercorns, crushed
1 cup dry white wine
4 small mackerel

Put the tomato halves in a soup pan with the water, onion, garlic crushed with salt, bay leaf, marjoram, lemon rind, peppercorns and wine. Cover and bring to the boil. Cook for 10 minutes. Wash and clean the mackerel. Fillet them, but do not skin them. Cut each fillet into three and add to the pan. Add a little water or wine if necessary. The pieces of fish should be just covered. Simmer for 15 minutes, season with salt and serve.

PASTA, RICE AND PIZZA

Spaghetti alla napoletana

Spaghetti alla Napoletana

4 tablespoons olive oil
1 clove garlic, chopped
2 lb tomatoes, skinned, seeded and chopped
½ cup water
salt, pepper, sugar, dried basil
2 cups spaghetti
sprigs parsley
½ cup grated Parmesan cheese

Heat the oil in a pan. Add the garlic and tomatoes and fry for 5 minutes, stirring. Add the water, cover and stew over a low heat for 20 minutes. Season to taste with salt, pepper, sugar and basil.

Meanwhile cook the spaghetti in plenty of boiling salted water for 10 to 12 minutes until tender. Drain. Put into a hot dish, pour the tomato sauce into the centre, garnish with parsley and serve the grated Parmesan cheese separately.

Spaghetti alla Caprese

4 tablespoons olive oil
1 lb tomatoes, skinned and quartered
salt, pepper
2 cups spaghetti
1½ tbs butter
½ cup grated Emmenthal cheese
½ cup grated Parmesan cheese

FISH PASTE
2 tablespoons olive oil
1 oz anchovy fillets, soaked and drained
8 black olives, pitted and chopped
5 oz canned tuna
1 teaspoon lemon juice

Heat the oil in a pan, add the tomatoes, season with salt and pepper. Stew, covered, over a low heat for 20 minutes, stirring occasionally. Cook the spaghetti in plenty of boiling salted water for 10 to 12 minutes until tender. Drain.

Meanwhile make the fish paste. Warm the olive oil in a pan (but do not let it get really hot). Add the anchovies, olives, tuna with its oil, and lemon juice. Warm over a low heat but do not allow to fry. Mash the ingredients to make a paste.

Heat the butter in a pan and toss the spaghetti quickly in it. Serve the spaghetti in individual soup plates, pouring the tomato sauce on top, and placing some of the fish paste in the middle of each serving. Mix the cheeses in a small bowl and hand separately.

Spaghetti alla marinara

Spaghetti alla Marinara

1¼ lb fillets of white fish
juice ½ lemon
salt, pepper, sugar
butter
2 small onions, chopped
1 stick celery, chopped
1 carrot, chopped
1 leek, chopped
1 tablespoon flour
1 cup dry white wine
1 cup stock
2 tbs shelled mussels, drained
1 lb tomatoes, skinned, seeded and chopped
1 tablespoon chopped parsley
2 cups spaghetti
½ cup grated Parmesan cheese

Rinse the fish fillets in cold water, pat dry with absorbent paper. Dice the fish, place in a shallow bowl and trickle the lemon juice over it. Season with salt. Melt the butter in a pan, add the chopped vegetables and sauté for 3 to 5 minutes. Add the fish, dust with flour, stir, add the wine and stock. Simmer gently for 5 minutes. Season with salt and pepper and a pinch of sugar. Add the mussels, tomatoes and parsley. Cover and cook for 10 minutes.

Meanwhile cook the spaghetti in plenty of boiling salted water for 10 to 12 minutes until tender. Drain and put into a hot dish. Pour the fish and sauce over the spaghetti and sprinkle with grated cheese.

Spaghetti alla carbonara

Spaghetti alla Carbonara

2 cups spaghetti
3 tbs butter
2 cloves garlic, peeled
½ cup bacon, finely diced
½ cup light cream

3 eggs
3 egg yolks
1 tablespoon chopped parsley
½ cup grated Parmesan cheese
salt, black pepper

Cook the spaghetti in plenty of boiling salted water for 10 to 12 minutes until tender. Melt the butter in a pan, fry the garlic cloves for 3 minutes, then remove them from the pan. Add the bacon and fry for 5 minutes. Stir in the cream, bring to the boil, cover and remove from the heat. Beat the eggs and egg yolks in a bowl with the parsley and grated cheese. Drain the spaghetti. Add to the hot bacon and cream mixture. Pour the beaten eggs over it and mix all well together. Season to taste with salt. Place on individual dishes and grind black pepper over each serving.

Macaroni Amatrice

Macaroni Amatrice

¼ cup bacon, chopped
1 small onion chopped
5 tablespoons olive oil
5 cups canned tomatoes, chopped
2 cloves garlic, finely chopped
salt
¼ teaspoon sugar
¼ teaspoon chilli powder
½ teaspoon paprika
2 teaspoons dried basil
½ teaspoon dried oregano
2 cups short macaroni
1 oz provolone or other crumbly cheese

Fry the bacon until the fat runs. Add the onion and fry until soft. Add the oil and heat it. Add the tomatoes with the liquid from their can, and the garlic. Add the salt, sugar, chilli powder, paprika, basil and oregano and cook over a medium heat, with the pan uncovered, for 20 minutes.

Meanwhile cook the macaroni in plenty of boiling salted water for about 15 minutes until tender. Drain and put into a hot dish. Take the sauce off the heat, crumble the cheese and stir it into the sauce. Pour the sauce over the macaroni and serve.

Spaghetti alla Bolognese

3 tablespoons olive oil
1 onion, finely chopped
⅛ celeriac root, finely chopped
1 carrot, finely chopped
1 clove garlic, crushed
salt, pepper
1 lb ground beef
2 teaspoons flour
4 tablespoons red wine
¾ lb canned tomatoes
1 tablespoon tomato paste
½ cup stock
1 bay leaf
2 cups spaghetti
½ cup grated Parmesan cheese

Heat the oil, fry the chopped vegetables and the garlic crushed with salt, than add the minced beef and fry until golden brown. Dust with flour and stir well. Add the wine and bring to the boil. Break up the tomatoes with a wooden spoon and add them with their juice to the pan. Add the tomato paste, stock, bay leaf and seasoning. Simmer, covered, over a gentle heat for 50 minutes, stirring from time to time. Remove the bay leaf before serving. Meanwhile cook the spaghetti in plenty of boiling salted water for 10 to 12 minutes until tender. Drain. Put in a hot dish, pour the sauce over it and sprinkle with Parmesan cheese.

Macaroni alla fiorentina

Macaroni alla Siciliana

½ cup olive oil
2 eggplants, diced
3 tomatoes, skinned, seeded and roughly chopped
2 cloves garlic, finely minced
salt, pepper, cayenne, grated nutmeg
½ teaspoon each dried thyme, basil
1 cup long macaroni
½ lb ground beef
2 onions, chopped
3 tablespoons red wine
½ cup grated Parmesan cheese
1½ tbs butter

Heat half the oil in a pan, add the eggplant, tomatoes and garlic and stew for 5 minutes. Shake the pan from time to time so that the vegetables do not stick. Season with salt, pepper, cayenne, nutmeg, thyme and basil. Cover and leave to stew for 15 minutes. Cook the macaroni in plenty of boiling salted water for about 15 minutes until tender. Drain.

Meanwhile heat the remaining oil in a pan, add the ground beef and chopped onions and fry for 10 minutes, stirring. Add the red wine and cook for 3 minutes more, then turn into the vegetable mixture and mix all well together.

Grease an ovenproof dish and put the macaroni into it. Mix in half the cheese. Place the vegetable and meat mixture on top of the macaroni and put the rest of the cheese and the butter, divided into flakes, on top of that. Brown for 5 minutes in the oven at 425°.

Macaroni alla Fiorentina

2 tbs butter
1 cup ham, diced
1 onion, finely chopped
1 carrot, grated
¼ celeriac root, grated
1 lb ground beef
½ cup dry white wine
6 oz canned tomato paste
salt, pepper, ground cloves, grated nutmeg
1 cup long macaroni
1 cup grated Parmesan cheese
tomato catsup
sprigs parsley

Melt the butter in a pan and fry the ham for 2 minutes. Add the onion, carrot and celeriac and fry for 3 minutes. Add the ground beef and cook for 5 minutes. Stir in the wine and tomato paste, and cook for another 10 minutes. Season with salt, pepper, ground cloves and grated nutmeg. Meanwhile cook the macaroni in plenty of boiling salted water for about 15 minutes until tender. Drain.

Grease an ovenproof dish with butter. Put in a layer of macaroni, then a layer of filling, then a sprinkling of Parmesan cheese. Repeat until all the ingredients are used up, finishing with a layer of Parmesan. Bake at 425° for 20 minutes. Turn out on to a hot plate and pour over some tomato catsup. Garnish with parsley.

Apulian Noodles

Apulian noodles

4 tablespoons olive oil
1 lb tomatoes, roughly chopped
1 onion, quartered
1 carrot, chopped
1 stick celery, chopped
1 leek, chopped
2½ cups stock
4 tbs flour
1½ cups ribbon noodles
½ cup butter
2 tbs breadcrumbs
3 tablespoons chopped pine nuts
1 tablespoon sugar

To make the sauce, heat the oil and sauté the vegetables briefly in it. Add a little stock and simmer for 15 minutes. Pass through a sieve. Make up to 3 cups with stock. Mix the flour with a little cold water and use to bind the sauce. Allow to simmer for 7 minutes. Keep the sauce hot.

Cook the noodles in plenty of boiling salted water for about 10 minutes until tender. Drain and arrange in a hot dish. Pour the tomato sauce over them and keep hot. Melt the butter in a frying pan, add the breadcrumbs, chopped pine nuts and sugar, and brown lightly. Scatter over the noodles.

Noodles with herb sauce

Noodles with Herb Sauce

2 cups wide ribbon noodles
2 cloves garlic, peeled
3 tbs pine nuts, chopped
3 tablespoons chopped basil
1 tablespoon chopped marjoram
1 tablespoon olive oil
1 tablespoon warm water
salt
4 oz ricotta cheese
2 tablespoons light cream
2 tbs butter

Cook the noodles in plenty of boiling salted water for about 10 minutes until tender. Meanwhile put the garlic and pine nuts into a mortar and crush them. Transfer them to a bowl and mix with the basil and marjoram. Stir in the oil and water and season with salt. Mash the cheese with a fork, add to the herb mixture with the cream. Stir until smooth. Drain the noodles, return them to the pan and toss in the butter. Place on a hot dish and serve with the herb sauce poured over.

Shell pasta in tomato sauce

Lasagne

2½ cups milk
1 bay leaf
1 tablespoon olive oil
1 onion, chopped
¾ lb ground beef
1 carrot, chopped
1½ cups stock
1 tablespoon tomato paste
salt, pepper, oregano
¾ cup green lasagne
2 tbs butter
3 tbs flour
¼ cup grated Parmesan cheese

Heat the milk and bay leaf together, remove from the heat, cover and set aside. Heat the oil in a large saucepan and fry the onion until softened. Add the ground beef and fry until browned. Add the carrot, stock and tomato paste, and season with salt, pepper and oregano. Cover and simmer over a low heat for 30 minutes. Adjust seasoning.

Meanwhile bring a large pan of water to the boil, add salt and a few drops of oil. Add the lasagne one piece at a time. Cook for 10 to 15 minutes until tender, then drain.

While the lasagne is cooking, make the béchamel sauce. Remove the bay leaf from the milk. Melt the butter in a saucepan, stir in the flour and cook for 2 minutes without browning. Add the milk gradually, stirring constantly. Simmer for 5 minutes.

Grease a shallow ovenproof dish. Line the dish with a layer of lasagne, pour on a little of the meat sauce and then a little of the béchamel sauce. Repeat these layers, ending with a layer of lasagne and a final layer of béchamel sauce. Sprinkle on the grated Parmesan cheese and bake at 400° for about 30 minutes until the top is lightly browned.

Shell Pasta in Tomato Sauce

½ cup bacon, diced
1 onion, chopped
1 clove garlic, crushed
salt, pepper, sugar
1 carrot, cut into cubes
1 bunch of celery, trimmed and cut into cubes
2 tomatoes, skinned, seeded and chopped
1 cup stock
½ cup dry white wine
2 tablespoons tomato paste
2 tbs butter
1 tablespoon chopped parsley
1¼ cups shell pasta
½ cup grated Parmesan cheese

Fry the bacon in a pan until the fat runs, add the onion and the garlic minced with salt, and fry for 5 minutes until golden. Add the carrot, celery and tomatoes. Pour in the stock and wine. Stir in the tomato paste, season with salt, pepper and a pinch of sugar. Cook over a moderate heat for 10 minutes. Add the butter and parsley.

Meanwhile cook the pasta in plenty of boiling salted water for 10 to 15 minutes until tender. Drain and add to the sauce. Heat through without boiling. Serve in a hot dish with Parmesan cheese sprinkled over.

Ravioli alla piemontese

Ravioli alla Piemontese

4 cups flour
5 eggs
1 tablespoon olive oil
salt
2 quarts stock
4 tbs butter, melted
½ cup grated Parmesan cheese

STUFFING
¼ cup bacon, finely diced
1 tablespoon olive oil
1 onion chopped
1 clove garlic, chopped
½ lb ground beef
½ cup red wine
½ cup stock
2 oz garlic sausage, skinned and finely diced
¼ teaspoon grated nutmeg
salt, pepper
1 lb spinach

Put the flour into a bowl, make a hollow in the middle, break the eggs into it and add the oil and a good pinch of salt. Gradually work in the flour with a fork. Mix to a paste. Turn on to a lightly floured surface and knead until smooth. Divide the paste in two and leave to rest for 1 hour in a bowl covered by a damp cloth.

Meanwhile prepare the stuffing. Fry the bacon in a pan until the fat runs. Add the oil and heat it. Add the onion and garlic and fry gently over a low heat until they begin to soften. Add the ground beef and fry over a higher heat, stirring, for 5 minutes. Pour in the wine. Stew for 20 minutes, until the liquid has evaporated, then pour in the stock. Add the diced sausage. Season with nutmeg, salt and pepper. Cover and cook for 10 minutes longer over a low heat.

Meanwhile rinse and pick over the spinach. Cook until tender without any additional water except that which clings to the leaves. Chop the spinach finely. Mix with the meat.

Roll out half the paste very thinly on a floured board. Put little mounds of stuffing on it about 1½ inches apart. Roll out the second half of the paste and place over the first. Using a notched wheel-type cookie cutter, cut out 1½ inch squares. Press the edges of the paste well together with your fingers.

Bring the stock to the boil in a large pan and put in the ravioli. Allow them to simmer very gently, uncovered, for 15 to 20 minutes. Take them out with a slotted spoon and put them on a hot dish. Pour melted butter over them and sprinkle with grated Parmesan cheese.

Calabrian Polenta

2½ cups salted water
2 cups corn meal
2 tbs butter
SAUCE
2 tablespoons olive oil
1 onion, chopped
2 cloves garlic, minced
salt, pepper
1 lb tomatoes, skinned and quartered
½ cup stock
1 large ham bone
1 bay leaf
3 peppercorns
1 teaspoon sugar
¼ teaspoon dried thyme
¾ cup grated Parmesan cheese

To make the polenta, bring the salted water to the boil in a large pan. Pour in the corn meal, stirring. Add the butter. Cook over a low heat for 5 minutes, stirring all the time so that the flour does not stick. Then cover and leave to thicken for 30 minutes over the lowest possible heat.

Meanwhile make the sauce. Heat the oil in a pan. Fry the onion and the garlic minced with salt for 5 minutes. Add the tomatoes, fry for another 5 minutes, stirring. Add the stock, ham bone, bay leaf and peppercorns. Cover and cook for 25 minutes. Remove the ham bone, put the sauce through a sieve and season with sugar, pepper and thyme.

Cover the base of a hot deep dish with some of the sauce, sprinkle a little cheese on top and spoon over a layer of polenta. Repeat these layers until the polenta is used up, finishing with layers of sauce and cheese. Serve at once.

Baked Gnocchi

2 cups milk
⅔ cup semolina
salt, pepper, grated nutmeg
1¼ cups grated Parmesan cheese
1 egg yolk, beaten

Gnocchi are dumplings, made of semolina or sometimes potato. They are served with meat or fish dishes.

Grease a cookie sheet. Heat the milk in a pan. Sprinkle in the semolina. Season with salt, pepper and nutmeg. Cook gently, stirring, for 10 to 15 minutes. Remove from the heat, stir in 1 cup grated cheese. Spread the semolina mixture on the cookie sheet, about ¾ inch thick. Leave to cool.

Cut out half-moon or diamond shapes and place in a shallow ovenproof dish. Brush with beaten egg yolk. Scatter the remaining cheese over the top. Bake at 400° for 15 minutes.

Baked gnocchi

Risotto mould

Risotto Mould

5 tbs butter
1 onion, finely chopped
1 cup long-grain rice
2 cups stock
8 oz canned mushrooms
½ lb tomatoes, skinned, seeded and quartered
salt, pepper
⅓ cup grated Parmesan or Emmenthal cheese
sprigs parsley

Heat 3 tbs butter in a pan and fry the onion for 5 minutes until it begins to soften. Add the rice and fry, stirring, for about 3 minutes, until it begins to look transparent. Pour in the stock. Cover and simmer gently for about 20 minutes, until the rice is tender and has absorbed all the liquid.

Reserve a few of the mushrooms for the garnish and slice the remainder. Heat the remaining butter in another pan and cook the tomatoes and sliced mushrooms for 5 minutes. Season with salt and pepper. Mix the rice gently with the tomatoes, mushrooms and grated cheese, Press into a smooth round bowl, then turn out on to a hot dish. Garnish with the reserved mushrooms and sprigs of parsley.

Risotto alla Milanese

4 tablespoons olive oil
1 onion, finely chopped
1¼ cups rice
2½ cups chicken stock
salt, pepper
2 tbs butter
½ cup grated Emmenthal cheese
½ cup grated Parmesan cheese

Heat the oil in a pan and fry the onion for about 5 minutes until it starts to soften. Add the rice and fry, stirring, for about 3 minutes until it begins to look transparent. Pour in the stock. Season with salt and pepper, cover and cook over a gentle heat for about 20 minutes, until the rice is tender and has absorbed all the liquid. Stir with a fork, mix in the butter and grated cheeses and serve in a hot dish.

Risotto alla Napoletana

1 cup bacon, diced
2 onions, finely chopped
1¼ cups short-grain rice
3 cups stock
1 bay leaf
salt, pepper, dried thyme
¾ lb tomatoes
2 tablespoons chopped parsley
1 cup grated Parmesan cheese

Fry the bacon gently in a pan until the fat runs. Add the onions and fry for 5 minutes until they begin to soften. Add the rice and fry, stirring, for 3 minutes until it begins to look transparent. Add the stock, bay leaf, salt and pepper. Bring to the boil, cover and simmer over a low heat for about 20 minutes, until the rice is tender and has absorbed all the liquid.

Reserve 1 tomato for garnishing. Skin, seed and chop the remainder and mix with a pinch of thyme. Add to the rice after it has been cooking for 10 minutes. Slice the reserved tomato. To serve, garnish the risotto with chopped parsley and tomato slices and hand the grated cheese separately.

Risotto alla napoletana

Vegetable Risotto

½ cup olive oil
1 onion, finely chopped
1 clove garlic, minced
1 red pepper, seeded and chopped
1 green pepper, seeded and chopped
1 cup rice
salt, paprika, sugar
2½ cups water
½ lb frozen peas
6 oz mushrooms, chopped
2 tbs butter
6 oz canned carrots, chopped
½ lb tomatoes, skinned, seeded and chopped
⅓ cup grated Parmesan or Emmenthal cheese

Heat the oil in a pan. Fry the onion, garlic and peppers for 5 minutes until they begin to soften. Add the rice and fry, stirring, for about 3 minutes until it begins to look transparent. Season with salt, paprika and sugar. Gradually pour in the water. Cover and cook gently over a low heat for about 20 minutes, until the rice is tender and has absorbed all the water. The grains of rice should remain separate, so do not stir, just shake the pan from time to time.

Cook the peas separately in boiling salted water for 5 minutes, then drain. Fry the mushrooms in the butter, then drain. Add the peas, mushrooms, carrots and tomatoes to the rice and heat through. Finally stir in the grated cheese.

Right: Vegetable risotto

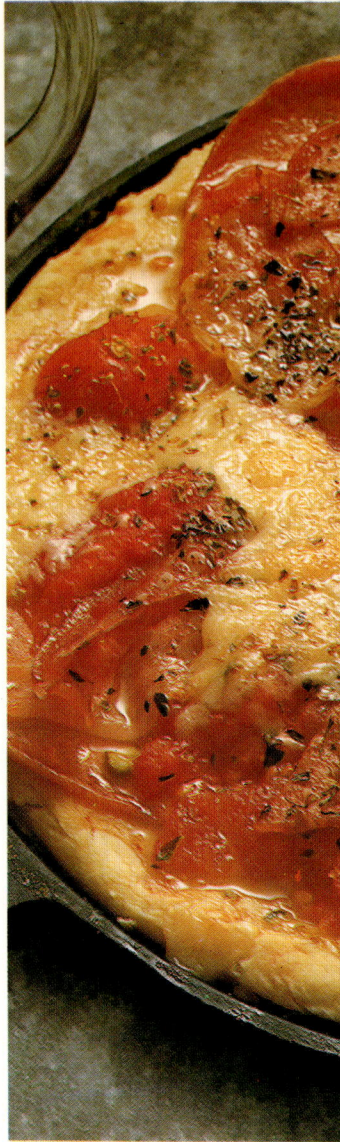

Right: Mortadella pizza

Anchovy pizza

Anchovy Pizza

¼ oz fresh yeast or 1 teaspoon dried yeast
sugar
about ½ cup lukewarm water
2 cups flour
½ teaspoon salt

TOPPING
¾ lb canned tomatoes, drained and chopped
2 oz mozzarella cheese, cut into pieces
½ cup bacon, diced
1 onion, chopped
2 oz anchovy fillets, soaked and drained
6 stuffed olives, sliced
¼ teaspoon dried oregano

To make the dough, mix the fresh yeast with a pinch of sugar and a little of the water, then add the remaining water. (If using dried yeast, dissolve ¼ teaspoon sugar in the water, sprinkle on the yeast and stir well.) Leave to stand in a warm place for about 10 minutes. Meanwhile sift the flour and salt into a bowl. Make a hollow in the centre and pour in the yeast mixture. Fold the flour over the yeast and mix, adding more water if necessary. Turn on to a lightly floured surface and knead for 10 minutes until you have a smooth dough. Return to the bowl, cover and leave in a warm place for about 1 hour until double in size.

Brush a pizza mould or 11 inch loose-based flan pan with oil. Roll out the dough to the size of the mould. Fit the dough into the mould, prick with a fork. Spread the tomatoes on the dough. Add the cheese, bacon and onion. Curl up the anchovy fillets and arrange on top with the sliced olives. Sprinkle on the oregano. Bake at 475° for 10 to 15 minutes.

Mortadella Pizza

¼ oz fresh yeast or 1 teaspoon dried yeast
sugar
about ½ cup lukewarm water
2 cups flour
½ teaspoon salt

TOPPING
½ lb mortadella sausage, skinned and thinly sliced
½ lb tomatoes, skinned and sliced
¼ lb ham, thinly sliced
2 eggs
salt, pepper
¼ teaspoon dried oregano
½ cup grated Parmesan cheese

To make the dough, mix the fresh yeast with a pinch of sugar and a little of the water, then add the remaining water. (If using dried yeast, dissolve ¼ teaspoon sugar in the water, sprinkle on the yeast and stir well.) Leave to stand in a warm place for about 10 minutes. Meanwhile sift the flour and salt into a bowl. Make a hollow in the centre and pour in the yeast mixture. Fold the flour over the yeast and mix, adding more water if necessary. Turn on to a lightly floured surface and knead for 10 minutes until you have a smooth dough. Return to the bowl, cover and leave in a warm place for about 1 hour until double in size.

Brush a pizza mould or 11 inch loose-based flan pan with oil. Roll out the dough to the size of the mould. Fit the dough into the mould, prick with a fork. Arrange the mortadella on the dough, then add the tomatoes and finally the gammon. Beat the eggs with the seasoning and oregano, and pour over the pizza. Sprinkle with the grated cheese and bake at 240°C/475°F/gas 9 for 10 to 15 minutes.

Pizza Giugliano (see overleaf)

¼ oz fresh yeast or 1 teaspoon dried yeast
sugar
about ½ cup lukewarm water
8 oz flour
½ teaspoon salt

TOPPING
3 tablespoons olive oil
2 cloves garlic, minced
¾ lb canned tomatoes drained and coarsely chopped
salt, pepper, grated nutmeg
¼ teaspoon mild paprika
2 drops Tabasco sauce
1 teaspoon dried basil
⅛ teaspoon baking soda
1 tablespoon anchovy paste
3 oz canned mushrooms, sliced
2 oz lean cooked ham, thinly sliced
2 oz mozzarella cheese, thinly sliced
1 oz anchovy fillets soaked and drained
1 teaspoon dried oregano

To make the dough, cream the fresh yeast with a pinch of sugar and a little of the water, then add the remaining water. (If using dried yeast, dissolve ¼ teaspoon sugar in the water, sprinkle on the yeast and stir well.) Leave to stand in a warm place for about 10 minutes. Meanwhile sift the flour and salt into a bowl. Make a hollow in the centre and pour in the yeast mixture. Fold the flour over the yeast and mix, adding more water if necessary. Turn on to a lightly floured surface and knead for 10 minutes until you have a smooth dough. Return to the bowl, cover and leave in a warm place for about 1 hour until double in size.

Meanwhile make the sauce. Heat 2 tablespoons oil in a pan. Add the garlic, tomatoes, salt, pepper, grated nutmeg, paprika, Tabasco sauce, basil and baking soda. Bring to the boil and simmer gently for 15 minutes.

Brush a pizza mould or 11 inch loose-based flan pan with oil. Roll out the dough to the size of the mould. Fit the dough into the mould, prick with a fork. Mix the anchovy paste with the remaining oil. Spread thinly over the dough. Spread the tomato sauce evenly over the top. Add the mushrooms, ham, mozzarella and anchovy fillets and sprinkle with oregano. Bake at 475° for 10 to 15 minutes.

Overleaf: pizza Giugliano, tuna and egg salad

Pizza Dalida

SERVES 8

½ oz fresh yeast or 2 teaspoons dried yeast
sugar
about 1 cup lukewarm water
4 cups flour
1 teaspoon salt

TOPPING
½ cup butter
2 lb onions, sliced
2 cloves garlic, minced
2 tablespoons chopped parsley
½ teaspoon dried thyme
3 bay leaves, crushed
salt, pepper
24 black olives, halved and stoned
2 oz anchovy fillets, soaked and drained

To make the dough, mix the fresh yeast with a pinch of sugar and a little of the water, then add the remaining water. (If using dried yeast, dissolve ½ teaspoon sugar in the water, sprinkle on the yeast and stir well.) Leave to stand in a warm place for about 10 minutes. Meanwhile sift the flour and salt into a bowl. Make a hollow in the centre and pour in the yeast mixture. Fold the flour over the yeast and mix, adding more water if necessary. Turn on to a lightly floured surface and knead for 10 minutes until you have a smooth dough. Return to the bowl, cover and leave in a warm place for about 1 hour until double in size.

Meanwhile melt the butter in a pan. Add the onions, garlic, parsley, thyme and bay leaves. Cover and cook over a moderate heat for 10 minutes, until the onions are soft. Stir from time to time. Season with salt and pepper. Let the mixture cool.

Brush a 15 × 12 inch cookie sheet with oil. Roll out the dough to slightly larger than the size of the cookie sheet. Place on the sheet, pressing up the sides to make a raised rim. Prick the dough with a fork.

Put the olives on the dough and spread the onion mixture on top. Arrange the anchovy fillets over the pizza. Bake at 475° for 10 to 15 minutes.

Pizza alla napoletana

Pizza alla Napoletana

¼ oz fresh yeast or 1 teaspoon dried yeast
sugar
about ½ cup lukewarm water
2 cups flour
½ teaspoon salt

TOPPING
3 tablespoons olive oil
¾ lb canned tomatoes, drained and coarsely chopped
2 cloves garlic, minced
1 tablespoon sugar
salt, pepper
2 teaspoons dried basil
⅛ teaspoon baking soda
1 teaspoon anchovy paste
5 oz mozzarella cheese, diced
¼ teaspoon dried oregano

To make the dough, mix the fresh yeast with a pinch of sugar and a little of the water, then add the remaining water. (If using dried yeast, dissolve ¼ teaspoon sugar in the water, sprinkle on the yeast and stir well.) Leave to stand in a warm place for about 10 minutes. Meanwhile sift the flour and salt into a bowl. Make a hollow in the centre and pour in the yeast mixture. Fold the flour over the yeast and mix, adding more water if necessary. Turn on to a lightly floured surface and knead for 10 minutes until you have a smooth dough. Return to the bowl, cover and leave in a warm place for about 1 hour until double in size.

Meanwhile make the sauce. Heat 2 tablespoons oil in a pan. Add the garlic, tomatoes, sugar, salt, pepper, basil and baking soda. Bring to the boil and simmer for 15 minutes over a low heat. Brush a pizza mould or 11 inch loose-based flan pan with oil. Roll out the dough to slightly larger than the size of the mould. Fit the dough into the mould, pressing up the sides to make a raised rim. Prick the dough with a fork. Mix the anchovy paste with the remaining oil. Spread thinly over the dough. Spread the tomato sauce evenly over the top, add mozzrella and sprinkle with oregano. Bake at 475° for 10 to 15 minutes.

FISH AND SHELLFISH

Stuffed mackerel

Stuffed Mackerel

4 mackeral (approx 7 oz each)
juice 1 lemon
salt, pepper, cayenne, garlic powder
1 green pepper, seeded
2 onions, chopped
2 tomatoes, skinned, seeded and chopped
1 tablespoon chopped parsley
1 teaspoon anchovy paste
4 bay leaves
½ cup dry white wine
½ cup grated Parmesan cheese

Wash and clean the mackerel. Pat dry. Season inside and out with lemon juice, salt and pepper. Cut the green pepper into strips ¼ inch wide and ½ inch long. Mix with the onions, tomatoes and parsley, and season with cayenne, garlic powder and anchovy paste. Stuff the mackeral with this mixture, adding a bay leaf to each fish. Fasten the cut edges with cocktail sticks. Butter an ovenproof dish and put the fish in it. Pour over the wine and sprinkle with grated cheese. Bake at 400° for 15 minutes.

Baked Eel

1½ lb eel, cleaned
½ lb mussels
3 tablespoons olive oil
1 lb tomatoes skinned, seeded and roughly chopped
3 tablespoons chopped parsley
1 onion, finely chopped
salt, pepper
⅓ cup dry white wine

Cut the eel into pieces 1½ inches thick. Scrub the mussels well under cold running water and remove the beards. Bring some lightly salted water to the boil in a pan. Add the mussels and cook, covered, over a high heat for 5 minutes. The mussels will open. Drain and remove the mussels from their shells.

Pour the oil into an ovenproof dish. Add the pieces of eel, the mussels, tomatoes and 2 tablespoons parsley. Sprinkle the onion, salt and pepper over the top. Add the wine. Cover and bake at 400° for 40 minutes. Serve with the remaining parsley scattered over the top.

Right: Baked eel

Ligurian fish casserole

Ligurian Fish Casserole

1¼ cups spaghetti
5 oz canned tuna, flaked
7 oz smoked halibut, boned and flaked
5 oz canned mushrooms, drained
½ lb tomatoes, sliced
½ cup sour cream
½ cup milk
2 eggs
½ cup grated Parmesan cheese
salt, pepper, garlic powder
1 tablespoon chopped parsley

Cook the spaghetti in plenty of boiling salted water for about 10 minutes until just tender. Drain. Butter an ovenproof dish, put in half the spaghetti. Add the tuna in a layer, then the halibut, then the mushrooms. Arrange the remaining spaghetti on top of the mushrooms. Top with the sliced tomatoes. Whisk the sour cream, milk, eggs and Parmesan together. Season well with salt, pepper, garlic powder and parsley. Pour over the fish and spaghetti mixture. Bake at 400° for 30 minutes.

Seafood Fritters

½ lb eel, cleaned, skinned and boned
½ lb fillets of sole
¼ lb frozen shrimp, thawed
½ lb canned mussels, drained
juice 1 lemon
salt, pepper
oil for deep frying
parsley sprigs
1 lemon sliced
1 tomato, cut into eighths

BATTER
3 eggs
4 tbs flour
salt, pepper
1 teaspoon each dried rosemary, basil

To make the batter, beat the eggs with a wire whisk and gradually add the flour and olive oil. Add salt, pepper, rosemary and basil. Leave to stand for 30 minutes.

Cut the eel into bite-sized pieces. Wash the sole and pat dry with absorbent paper. Sprinkle all the fish and shellfish with lemon juice. Season the eel, sole and shrimp with salt and pepper. Roll up the fillets of sole and fasten with cocktail sticks.

Dip the fish and shellfish in the batter and fry in hot oil for about 10 minutes. Drain on absorbent paper and place on a hot dish. Garnish with parsley, lemon and tomato, and serve with green sauce (see page 71).

Florentine Baked Fish

4 pieces fillet of cod (¼ lb each)
juice 1 lemon
1 lb spinach, washed and picked over
salt, pepper
½ lb potatoes, boiled in their skins, peeled and sliced
1 lb tomatoes, skinned, seeded and chopped
1 clove garlic, minced
½ cup stock
½ cup grated Parmesan cheese
3 tbs butter

Rinse the pieces of cod under cold water, pat dry, trickle lemon juice over them. Butter an ovenproof dish, place the spinach in it, arrange the fish on top and season with salt. Place the potato slices round the edge and the chopped tomatoes and garlic over the fish. Pour over the stock. Season with pepper and scatter over the grated cheese. Add the butter, divided into small flakes. Bake at 425° for 20 minutes.

Sicilian anchovies

Sicilian Anchovies

1¾ lb fresh anchovies or whiting
salt, pepper, dried basil
2 tablespoons olive oil
1 onion, chopped
1 clove garlic, minced
¾ lb canned tomatoes, drained
¼ lb provolone or other crumbly cheese
1 tablespoon capers
8 canned anchovy fillets, soaked and drained

Wash and clean the fresh anchovies or sprats, removing heads and tails. Pat dry. Season with salt and pepper both inside and out. To make the tomato sauce, heat the oil in a pan, fry the onion and garlic until they begin to soften. Add the tomatoes and cook over a high heat until the sauce is well reduced. Season with salt and pepper and a pinch of basil.

Grease an ovenproof dish. Put a layer of fish in the dish. Cover with half the sauce and scatter with half the cheese. Add half the capers and all the canned anchovy fillets. Now add the remaining fish, sauce, cheese and capers, in layers as before. Bake at 425° for 20 minutes.

Baked Mussels

4 lb mussels
1 cup water
1 cup dry white wine
1 bay leaf
3 onions, peeled
2 cloves
salt, pepper
¾ lb tomatoes, skinned, seeded and chopped
2 cloves garlic, minced
½ cup light cream
juice 1 lemon
1 teaspoon Worcestershire sauce
½ cup grated Parmesan cheese
½ cup grated Emmenthal cheese
8 sprigs parsley
4 tbs butter

Scrub the mussels well under cold running water and remove the beards. Boil up the water and wine in a large pan, add the bay leaf and 1 onion with the cloves stuck into it. Season with salt and pepper. When the liquid is boiling hard, add the mussels, cover the pan and cook for 5 minutes. Drain, reserving the liquid, and remove the mussels from their shells. Place in a shallow ovenproof dish.

Chop the remaining onions. Cover the mussels with the tomatoes, onions and garlic. Strain ½ cup of the reserved cooking liquid through a sieve into a bowl, beat up with the cream, lemon juice, Worcestershire sauce, salt and pepper and pour over the mussels. Scatter the cheese down the centre of the dish and put pieces of parsley down the sides. Dab with the butter divided into flakes. Bake at 425° for 10 minutes.

Baked mussels

Trout with Mushrooms

4 trout (½ lb each)
juice 1 lemon
salt, pepper
flour for coating
4 tablespoons oil

½ lb mushrooms
3 tbs breadcrumbs
1 tablespoon chopped parsley
1½ tbs butter

Wash and clean the trout. Pat dry, season inside and out with lemon juice, salt and pepper. Turn in the flour. Heat the oil in a large frying pan and fry the trout for 2 minutes on each side. Keep warm on a plate. Butter an ovenproof dish. Put the mushrooms on the bottom of the dish and lay the trout on top of them. Sprinkle the breadcrumbs over the trout. Scatter the parsley over the dish. Add the butter, divided into small flakes. Bake at 400° for 15 minutes.

Deviled Shrimp

¾ lb frozen shrimp, thawed
juice 1 lemon
salt, pepper, chilli sauce, sugar
2 tablespoons olive oil
1 onion, chopped
2 cloves garlic, crushed
1 lb tomatoes, skinned, seeded and chopped

1 teaspoon dried oregano
½ teaspoon dried basil
½ cup stock
3 tbs butter
2 tablespoons brandy
1 tablespoon chopped parsley

Bring some lightly salted water to a boil in a pan. Add the shrimp and simmer for 1 minute. Drain and cool, place in a dish, sprinkle with lemon juice, pepper and a little chilli sauce. Mix carefully, cover and leave for 20 minutes to absorb the flavors.

   Heat the oil in a saucepan, add the onion and the garlic minced with salt. Fry gently until softened. Add the tomatoes and cook, stirring, for 10 minutes. Season well with salt, pepper, chilli sauce, sugar, oregano and basil. Add the stock, let all cook gently for 10 minutes longer. Keep the sauce hot without letting it boil.

   Heat the butter in a frying pan. Drain the shrimp and pat dry on absorbent paper. Fry until golden brown on all sides, about 5 minutes. Remove from the heat, pour over the brandy and set light to it. When the flames have died down, arrange the shrimp on a warm dish, salt slightly and pour over the tomato sauce. Scatter with parsley and serve.

Deviled shrimp

MEAT AND POULTRY

Sicilian Veal Roll

1½ lb boned leg of veal
salt, pepper
3 hard-cooked eggs, chopped
½ lb ham, diced
½ lb garlic sausage, skinned and chopped
1 teaspoon mustard
¼ teaspoon grated nutmeg
4 tablespoons olive oil
1 cup white wine
1 cup stock
2 tablespoons tomato paste
2 teaspoons cornstarch

Flatten the veal by beating between sheets of greaseproof paper. Season with salt and pepper. Mix the hard-cooked eggs, ham, sausage, mustard and nutmeg to make a stuffing. Spread this over the meat. Roll up the meat and fasten with strong thread.

Heat the oil in a roasting pan. Brown the meat on all sides for about 5 minutes. Gradually add the wine, cover and simmer gently over a low heat for 1 hour 10 minutes. Half way through the cooking time add the stock and tomato paste. Baste the meat frequently during cooking to keep it from drying out.

Take the veal out of the pan, remove the thread and place on a hot dish. Mix the cornstarch with a little cold water and add to the pan juices. Simmer for 2 minutes. Slice the veal roll and serve the sauce separately.

Osso Buco

2 lb shank of veal
4 tbs butter
1 onion, finely chopped
½ cup dry white wine
¾ lb canned tomatoes, chopped
½ cup stock
salt, pepper
3 tablespoons finely chopped parsley
grated rind 1 lemon
1 clove garlic, minced

Ask your butcher to saw the veal into 2 inch pieces. Melt the butter in a wide pan and fry the onion until softened. Add the pieces of meat and fry until browned, then stand them upright so that the marrow does not fall out during cooking. Add the wine and simmer for 5 minutes. Add the chopped tomatoes and their juice, and simmer for a further 5 minutes. Finally add the stock and seasoning, cover and cook over a low heat until the veal is tender, about 1½ hours.

To serve, mix together the parsley, lemon rind and garlic, and sprinkle over the veal.

Neapolitan Veal Stew

1 lb boned leg of veal
⅓ cup olive oil
1 onion, finely chopped
1 clove garlic, minced
1 green and 1 red pepper, seeded and sliced
¼ lb mushrooms, sliced
1 cup stock
1 anchovy fillet, soaked, drained and chopped
5 olives, chopped
4 tomatoes, skinned, seeded and chopped
salt, pepper, dried oregano

Cut the veal into thin strips. Heat the oil in a pan and fry the meat on all sides for 10 minutes. Take out of the pan and keep hot. Add the onion and garlic to the pan and sauté for 5 minutes. Add the green and red peppers, the mushrooms and stock and stew for 10 minutes. Add the anchovy, olives and tomatoes. Return the meat to the pan and season with salt, pepper and oregano. Stew for another 5 minutes, then serve.

Piedmontese braised veal

Piedmontese Braised Veal

2 lb loin of veal
salt, pepper
4 tbs butter
1 cup white wine
1 carrot, diced
¼ celeriac root, diced
1 small leek, thinly sliced

SAUCE
1½ tbs butter
¼ cup flour
½ cup milk
½ cup cream
¼ cup grated Parmesan cheese
salt, pepper, grated nutmeg

Rub salt and pepper into the veal. Melt the butter in a braising pan and brown the veal on all sides, about 15 minutes. Pour the wine over it and add the vegetables. Cover and braise for 1½ hours. Take the roast out of the pan, carve it and arrange on a hot dish. Keep hot.

To make the sauce, sieve the juices from the pan and measure off; bring to the boil in a small pan. Melt the butter in another pan, add the flour and cook gently for 2 minutes, stirring. Add the hot meat juices and the milk. Stir until the sauce is thick and smooth, and simmer for 5 minutes. Add the cream and Parmesan cheese, and stir until the cheese has melted. Season to taste with salt, pepper and nutmeg. Serve the meat with the sauce handed separately.

Milanese Roast Veal *(see overleaf)*

SERVES 8

3 lb rolled loin of veal
salt, pepper
2 cloves garlic, minced
⅓ cup butter
2 tablespoons chopped parsley
1 teaspoon each dried rosemary, marjoram
2 cups stock
1 teaspoon cornstarch
3 oz canned tomato paste

Rub pepper and garlic crushed with salt into the roast. Melt the butter in a roasting pan, brown the roast on all sides, 5 to 10 minutes. Sprinkle the parsley, rosemary and marjoram over the meat. Pour the stock into the pan. Roast at 400° for 1 hour 35 minutes.

Take the joint out of the pan and put on a hot dish. Mix the cornstarch with a little cold water, add the tomato paste and stir into the meat juices left in the pan. Bring the sauce to the boil and serve with the meat.

Overleaf: Milanese roast veal

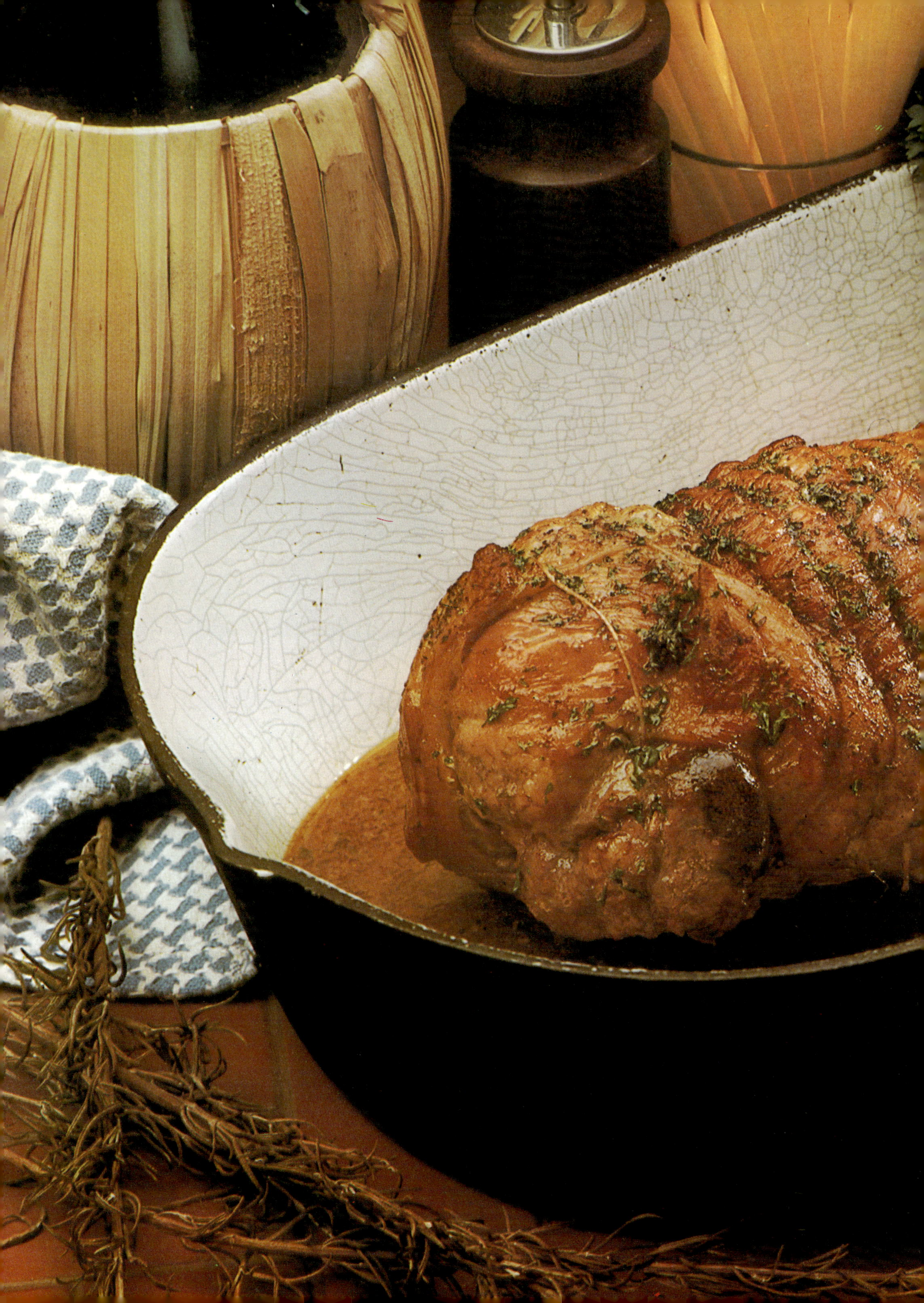

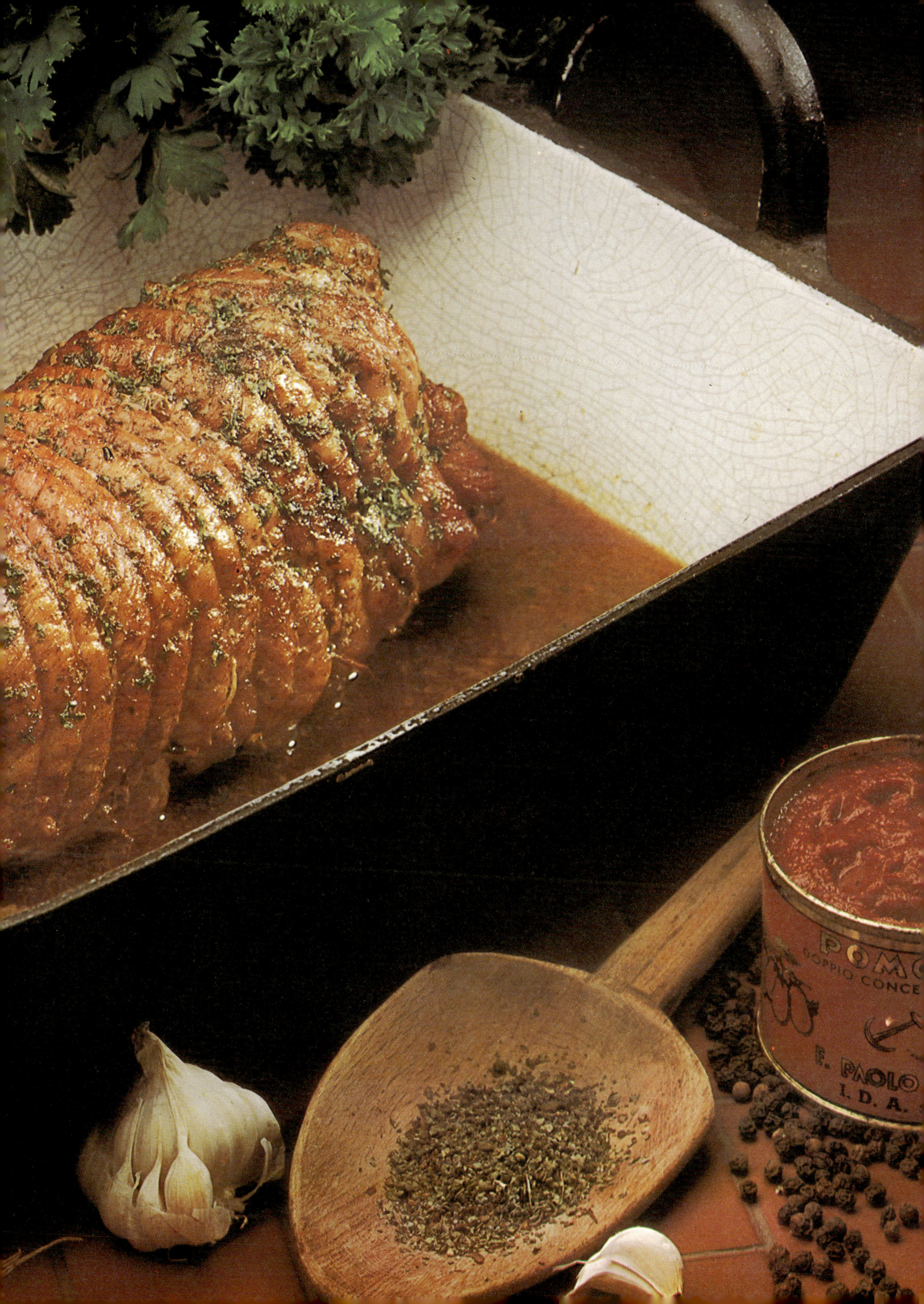
POMO
DOPPIO CONCE
F. PAOLO
I.D.A.

Veal Cutlets with Mozzarella

4 veal cutlets (½ lb each)
salt, pepper
1 egg
1 tablespoon evaporated milk
¼ cup grated Parmesan cheese
¼ cup breadcrumbs
flour for coating
oil for frying
4 tablespoons tomato catsup
4 slices mozzarella cheese (¼ lb)

Beat out the meat slightly between sheets of wax paper. Season with salt and pepper. Beat the egg and evaporated milk together. Mix the cheese and breadcrumbs together. Coat the cutlets first with flour, then with the egg mixture and finally with the breadcrumb mixture.

Heat some oil in a frying pan and fry the coated cutlets for 3 minutes on each side. Take them out of the pan, drain and place in a shallow ovenproof dish. Spread with tomato catsup and cover with the slices of cheese. Bake at 400° for 15 minutes.

Veal cutlets with mozzarella

Veal Scallops with Herbs

SERVES 6

2 teaspoons finely chopped sage
1 teaspoon finely chopped rosemary
salt, pepper
12 veal scallops (¼ lb each)
4 tbs butter
2 tablespoons finely chopped parsley
4 cloves garlic, minced
grated rind 2 lemons
½ cup dry white wine
½ cup stock

Mix the sage, rosemary, a little salt and pepper in a bowl. Scatter over the scallops and leave for 30 minutes to allow the flavours to be absorbed. Melt the butter in a frying pan and fry the meat for about 4 minutes on each side until golden brown. Remove from the pan and place on a hot dish. Mix the parsley, the garlic minced with salt and the grated lemon rind. Spread over the scallops and keep hot.

Pour the wine into the pan and bring to the boil, scraping up the meat juices. Simmer to reduce a little, then add the stock and return to the boil. Season the sauce with salt and pepper and pour over the veal. For a decorative effect, the scallops may be served speared on wooden skewers and garnished with sprigs of fresh herbs and lemon quarters, with the sauce handed separately.

Ticino Veal Scallops

4 veal scallops (¼ lb each)
juice ½ lemon
⅓ cup butter
1 onion, grated
1 clove garlic, minced
¾ lb tomatoes, skinned, seeded and chopped
1 tablespoon chopped parsley
1 teaspoon dried basil
½ teaspoon dried marjoram
½ cup grated Parmesan cheese
salt, pepper
2 small pickled cucumbers, finely chopped

Trickle lemon juice over the veal and leave to stand for 15 minutes. Melt half the butter in a saucepan, fry the onion and garlic until soft. Add the tomatoes and fry for another 5 minutes, stirring. Add the parsley, basil and marjoram. Sprinkle with cheese and season with salt and pepper, cover and cook gently for another 5 minutes over a low heat.

Melt the remaining butter in a frying pan. Season the veal scallops lightly with pepper and fry for about 4 minutes on each side. Take out of the pan, season lightly on both sides with salt, and arrange on a hot dish. Pour the juices from the frying pan and the tomato sauce over the veal. Arrange the pickled cucumbers in a broad strip over the center of the scallops.

Veal Scallops with Lemon (see overleaf)

4 veal scallops (¼ lb each)
salt, pepper
flour for coating
4 tbs butter
⅔ cup stock
1 lemon very thinly sliced
3 tablespoons dry white wine
1 tablespoon lemon juice
2 tablespoons chopped parsley
sprigs parsley

Season the scallops lightly with salt and pepper and coat them with flour, shaking off any excess flour. Melt the butter in a frying pan. Fry the veal for about 3 minutes on each side until golden brown. Remove from the pan, pour the stock into the pan and scrape up all the meat juices. Return the veal to the pan and place a slice of lemon on each scallop. (Keep back the remaining lemon slices for garnishing.) Simmer gently for 10 minutes. Take the veal out of the pan again, discarding lemon slices, and place on a hot dish. Cover and keep hot.

Add the wine to the pan juices and reduce the liquid by half. Strain the sauce into a saucepan. Mix in the lemon juice and just before the sauce reaches boiling point, mix in the parsley. Pour the sauce over the veal and garnish with the remaining lemon slices and sprigs of parsley.

Ticino veal scallops

Overleaf: veal scallops with lemon

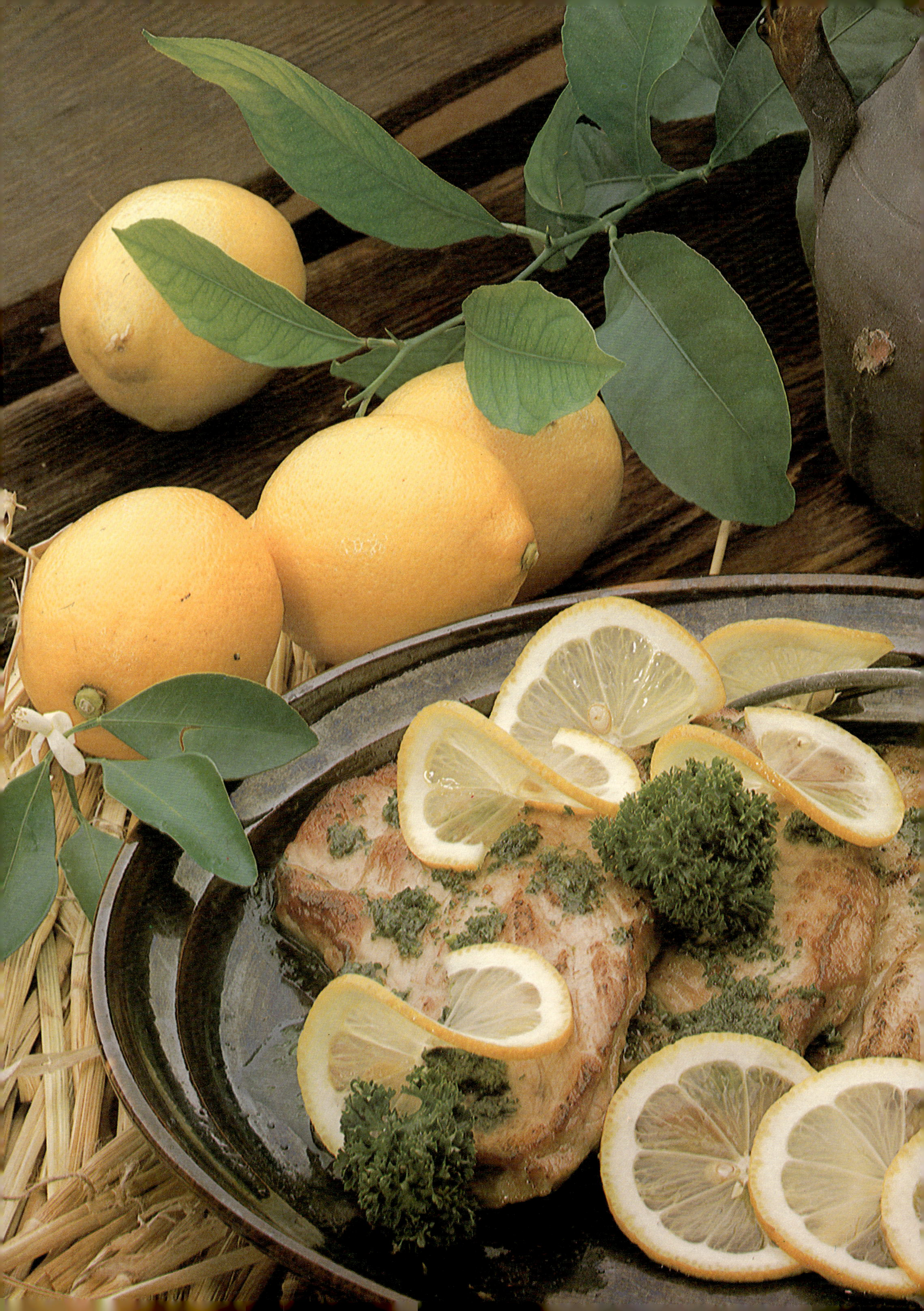

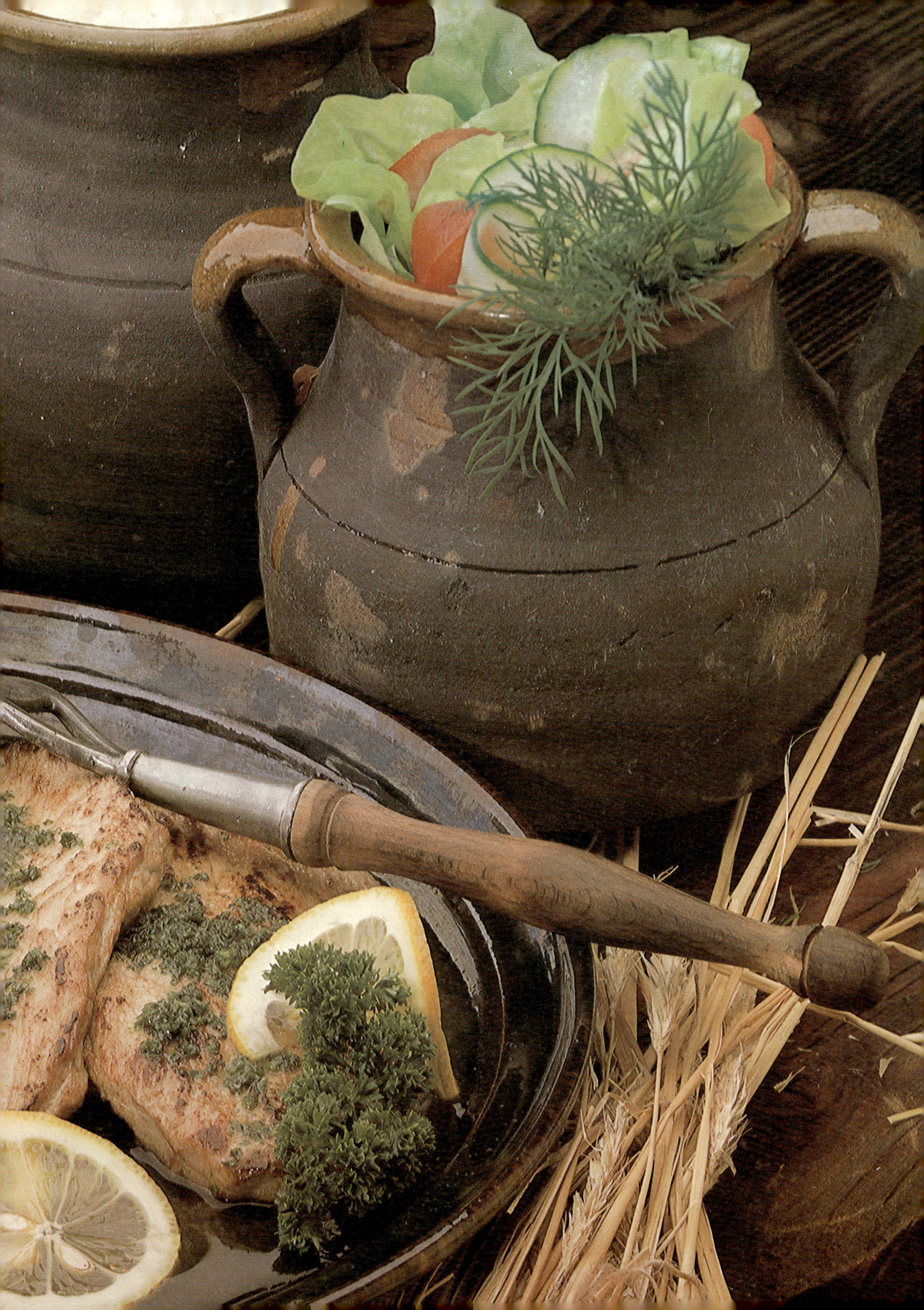

Milanese Veal Scallops

8 veal scallops (¼ lb each)
salt, pepper, paprika
1 egg
2 tablespoons evaporated milk
¼ cup grated Parmesan cheese
¼ cup breadcrumbs
4 tbs butter

SAUCE
2 tablespoons olive oil
¼ lb bacon, diced
¾ lb tomatoes, skinned, seeded and chopped
1 stalk celery, chopped
1 carrot, chopped
1 leek, chopped
1 clove garlic, minced
salt, pepper, baking soda, dried basil, oregano
5 oz canned tomato paste
1 cup water

To make the sauce, heat the oil in a pan and fry the bacon gently for 2 minutes. Add the tomatoes, chopped vegetables, garlic minced with salt, tomato paste and water. Simmer over a low heat for 30 minutes, stirring occasionally. Season well with salt, pepper, baking soda, basil and oregano. Cover and keep hot.

Beat out the scallops between sheets of wax paper. Season with salt, pepper and paprika. Beat the egg and milk together. Mix the grated cheese and breadcrumbs. Dip the scallops first in the egg mixture, then in the cheese and breadcrumb mixture. Melt the butter in a frying pan, and fry the meat for about 3 minutes on each side. Serve the sauce and meat on a bed of spaghetti.

Veal and pork scallops in Marsala sauce

Milanese veal scallops

Veal and Pork Scallops in Marsala Sauce

4 veal scallops (¼ lb each)
4 pork scallops (¼ lb each)
salt, pepper, curry powder
flour for coating
⅓ cup olive oil
5 tablespoons Marsala
1 cup stock
juice ½ lemon
1 canned pineapple ring, cut into eighths
4 cocktail cherries
sprigs parsley

Season the scallops with salt, pepper and curry powder and toss them in flour. Heat half the oil in a pan and fry the pork until golden brown, about 5 minutes each side. Take out and keep hot. Heat the remaining oil in the pan, fry the veal, about 4 minutes each side. Take out and keep hot.

Add the Marsala to the pan and scrape up the pan juices. Simmer for 5 minutes to reduce. Add the stock and lemon juice and bring to the boil. Adjust seasoning to taste. Arrange the meats on a hot dish, pour over a little of the sauce, and garnish with pieces of pineapple, cherries and parsley. Hand the rest of the sauce separately.

Braised beef with rosemary

Braised Beef with Rosemary

¼ cup bacon, finely diced
1 clove garlic, minced
  grated rind ½ lemon
salt, pepper
½ teaspoon dried rosemary
1½ lb loin of beef
½ cup flour
4 tablespoons olive oil
3 onions, sliced
½ cup red wine
½ cup water
1 tablespoon tomato paste
1 tablespoon light cream
1 tomato, quartered
  sprigs parsley

Mix the bacon, garlic, lemon rind, salt, pepper and rosemary. Rub into the meat. Cover the joint and put in the refrigerator for about 3 hours to absorb the flavours.

Dust the meat with half the flour. Heat the oil in a braising pan and fry the onions until they are golden yellow. Add the meat and fry on all sides until brown, about 10 minutes. Add the wine and water, stirring up any residue sticking to the pan. Cover and braise for 35 minutes over a low heat. Remove the meat from the pan, place on a hot dish, cover and keep warm.

To make the sauce, stir up the pan juices and sieve them into a saucepan. Bring to the boil. Mix the remaining flour with a little cold water and the tomato purée and add to the sauce. Bring to the boil, then simmer for 5 minutes over a low heat. Season with salt and pepper. Stir in the cream.

Garnish the meat with tomato quarters and parsley and serve the sauce separately.

Meatballs in Tomato Sauce

⅓ cup breadcrumbs
½ cup milk
1 lb ground beef
½ cup bacon, minced
1 clove garlic, minced
salt, pepper, ground allspice
1 tablespoon chopped parsley
2 eggs
¾ cup grated Parmesan cheese
grated rind 1 lemon
oil for frying
flour for coating

SAUCE
3 tablespoons olive oil
2 onions, chopped
¾ lb tomatoes, skinned, seeded and chopped
salt, pepper, dried basil, thyme, sugar
1½ cups stock

Soak the breadcrumbs in the milk, then drain, squeezing out excess liquid. Mix the breadcrumbs with the beef, bacon, garlic, salt, pepper, allspice, parsley, eggs, cheese and lemon rind. Shape into little balls about 1¼ inches across. Place side by side on a wooden board, cover with plastic wrap and put in the refrigerator to chill for 40 minutes.

Meanwhile make the sauce. Heat the oil in a pan and sauté the onions until they begin to soften. Add the tomatoes and cook over a high heat for 10 minutes. Season with salt, pepper, basil, thyme and sugar. Pour in the stock. Cover and simmer gently for 15 minutes. If you want an absolutely smooth sauce, you can put it through a strainer, keep hot.

To fry the meatballs, heat some oil in a frying pan. Roll the meatballs in flour and put half of them in the pan. Fry over moderate heat until golden brown on all sides, about 8 minutes. Keep turning them as you fry them, so that they keep their round shape. Take them out of the pan, drain and place on a hot dish. Add more oil to the pan and fry the remaining meatballs.

To serve, pour the hot tomato sauce over the meatballs.

Sirloin Steak in Wine Sauce

4 sirloin steaks (¼ lb each)
2 onions, finely chopped
1 clove garlic, minced
1 anchovy fillet, soaked, drained and finely chopped
1 tablespoon finely chopped parsley
½ teaspoon each dried rosemary, thyme
juice ½ lemon
3 tbs butter
salt, pepper, paprika
1 cup water
¼ cup flour
½ cup red wine
1 tablespoon light cream

Make incisions in the fat round the steaks so that the meat does not curl up while cooking. Mix the onions, garlic, anchovy, parsley, rosemary, thyme and lemon juice. Rub this mixture into the steaks. Cover and leave to absorb the flavors for 3 hours.

Melt the butter in a pan, and fry the steaks for 10 minutes over a low heat, turning once. Season with salt and pepper. Keep hot on a dish. To make the sauce, add the water to the pan and stir up the pan juices. Mix the flour with the wine and add to the sauce. Bring back to the boil. Simmer for 5 minutes over a low heat. Season with salt, pepper and paprika. Stir in the cream. Serve the meat with the sauce handed separately.

Roman Lamb Cutlets

¼ cup lentils, soaked and drained
¼ cup rice
4 lamb cutlets (¼ lb each)
salt, pepper, dried thyme
1½ tbs butter
4 tomatoes, seeded and sliced
½ cup stock
¼ cup grated Parmesan cheese

Cook the lentils in boiling salted water for 35 minutes. In another pan cook the rice in boiling salted water for 20 minutes. Season the cutlets with salt, pepper and thyme. Melt the butter in a frying pan and fry the cutlets for 4 minutes on each side. Drain and put aside. Drain the lentils and rice. Grease an ovenproof dish. Arrange the rice, sliced tomatoes and lentils in layers. Pour the stock over them and lay the cutlets on top. Cover and bake at 400° for 25 minutes. Sprinkle with grated cheese and serve.

Roman lamb cutlets

Spicy lamb cutlets

Spicy Lamb Cutlets

1 lb eggplant
salt, pepper
4 tbs butter
1 onion, chopped
1 clove garlic, minced
2 teaspoons curry powder
2 carrots, cubed
2 tablespoons tomato paste
½ cup water
¼ lb frozen peas
6 oz canned artichoke hearts, quartered
8 lamb cutlets (¼ lb each)

Slice the eggplant, and salt well on both sides. Leave on a board for 30 minutes to draw out the juice, then rinse and dry with absorbent paper.

Heat 3 tablespoons butter in a frying pan. Add the onion and the garlic minced with salt, and sauté for 5 minutes. Add the eggplant and sauté for another 5 minutes. Add the curry powder, carrots and tomato paste. Pour in the water and bring to the boil. Adjust seasoning to taste, cover and stew gently over a low heat for 20 minutes. After the first 10 minutes add the peas. After 15 minutes add the artichoke hearts.

Meanwhile heat the remaining butter in another frying pan. Rub salt and pepper into both sides of the cutlets and fry them for 4 minutes on either side. To serve, layer the vegetables and cutlets in a hot dish.

Lombard pork and vegetables

Lombard Pork and Vegetables

SERVES 6

2½ lb pork knuckle
4 tbs butter
½ cup dry white wine
½ cup stock
3 stalks celery
2 lb cabbage, finely shredded
1 lb carrots
salt, pepper
2 onions, chopped
6 pork chops (¼ lb each)
3 small garlic sausages (¼ lb each), halved

Wash the pork knuckle and pat dry with absorbent paper. Melt 1½ tbs butter in a saucepan and brown the pork knuckle on all sides, about 10 minutes. Pour in the wine and stock. Cut the celery into pieces ¾ inch long. Cut the carrots into rounds ½ inch thick. Add both to the pan, cover and cook slowly for 1 hour, adding more stock if necessary. Add the cabbage and cook slowly for a further 30 minutes. Season with salt and pepper.

Meanwhile, melt the remaining butter in a frying pan and gently fry the onions until softened. Push them to the side of the pan. Season the pork chops with salt and pepper, add to the pan and fry until crisp and brown, 10 minutes each side.

Add the halved garlic sausages to the stewpan to heat through. Then take the knuckle out of the pan, carefully remove the bones and cut the meat into thick slices. Put the vegetables in a hot dish and put the meat from the knuckle, the chops and the halved sausages on them.

Florentine chicken

Florentine Chicken

2½ lb chicken, quartered
salt, pepper, celery salt
2 tablespoons olive oil
1 onion, finely chopped
2 cloves garlic, minced
4 tomatoes, skinned, seeded and finely chopped
4 stuffed olives, chopped
¼ teaspoon dried thyme
½ teaspoon dried basil
¼ teaspoon dried marjoram or oregano
4 bay leaves

Season the chicken quarters with salt. Brush four large pieces of foil with oil, place the chicken quarters on them and pour the remaining oil over the chicken. Mix together the onion, garlic minced with salt, tomatoes, olives, thyme, basil, marjoram or oregano, pepper and celery salt. Spread this mixture on the chicken quarters and place a bay leaf on each. Fold the foil loosely over the chicken.

Place the chicken parcels on a rack set over a roasting pan and bake at 475° for 40 minutes. Open the foil and let the pieces of chicken go on cooking for another 15 minutes. Take out of the oven, remove the bay leaves, and serve the chicken in the foil wrappings.

Deep-fried Chicken

SERVES 8

2 chickens (3 lb each), quartered	1 teaspoon oil
salt	1 cup breadcrumbs
flour for coating	1 cup grated cheese
2 eggs	oil for deep frying
1 tablespoon milk	8 sprigs parsley
	1 lemon, sliced

Season the chicken quarters with salt and toss in flour. Beat together the eggs, milk and oil. Mix together the breadcrumbs and grated cheese. Dip the chicken quarters first into the egg mixture and then into the breadcrumb mixture.

Heat the oil for deep frying. Fry the chicken quarters for 20 minutes, until golden brown. Drain on absorbent paper. Fry the parsley for 2 minutes. Arrange the chicken on a dish with the parsley and lemon slices. Serve with tomato sauce (see Meatballs in Tomato Sauce, page 48).

Milanese Turkey

SERVES 6

5 lb turkey	½ lb liver pâté
salt, pepper	1 egg
⅔ cup butter	2 tablespoons rum
1 cup stock	½ cup milk
2 cups short macaroni	1 tablespoon lemon juice
½ lb cooked ham	grated rind ½ lemon
	salt, pepper

STUFFING
1 lb canned chestnuts

Season the turkey inside and out with salt and pepper.

To make the stuffing, crush the chestnuts lightly with a fork. Add the liver pâté, egg, rum, milk, lemon juice and rind. Mix well together and season to taste with salt and pepper. Stuff the turkey with this mixture. Sew up the neck and stomach openings, tie the wings and drumsticks to the body with string.

Put the turkey in a roasting pan, melt ⅓ cup butter in a saucepan and pour over the bird. Roast at 400° for 2½ hours. When the juices from the turkey begin to turn brown, add ½ cup stock to the pan. Baste the bird with the juices from time to time. Gradually add the rest of the stock. Ten minutes before the end of roasting time, brush the skin of the bird with salted water so that it will be really crisp. Strain the pan juices and serve separately.

Cook the macaroni in plenty of boiling salted water for about 15 minutes until tender. Meanwhile cut the ham into narrow strips. Drain the macaroni. Melt the remaining butter in a pan. Toss the macaroni and ham in the melted butter.

Place the turkey on a hot dish. Surround with the macaroni. Sieve the pan juices and serve separately.

Deep-fried chicken

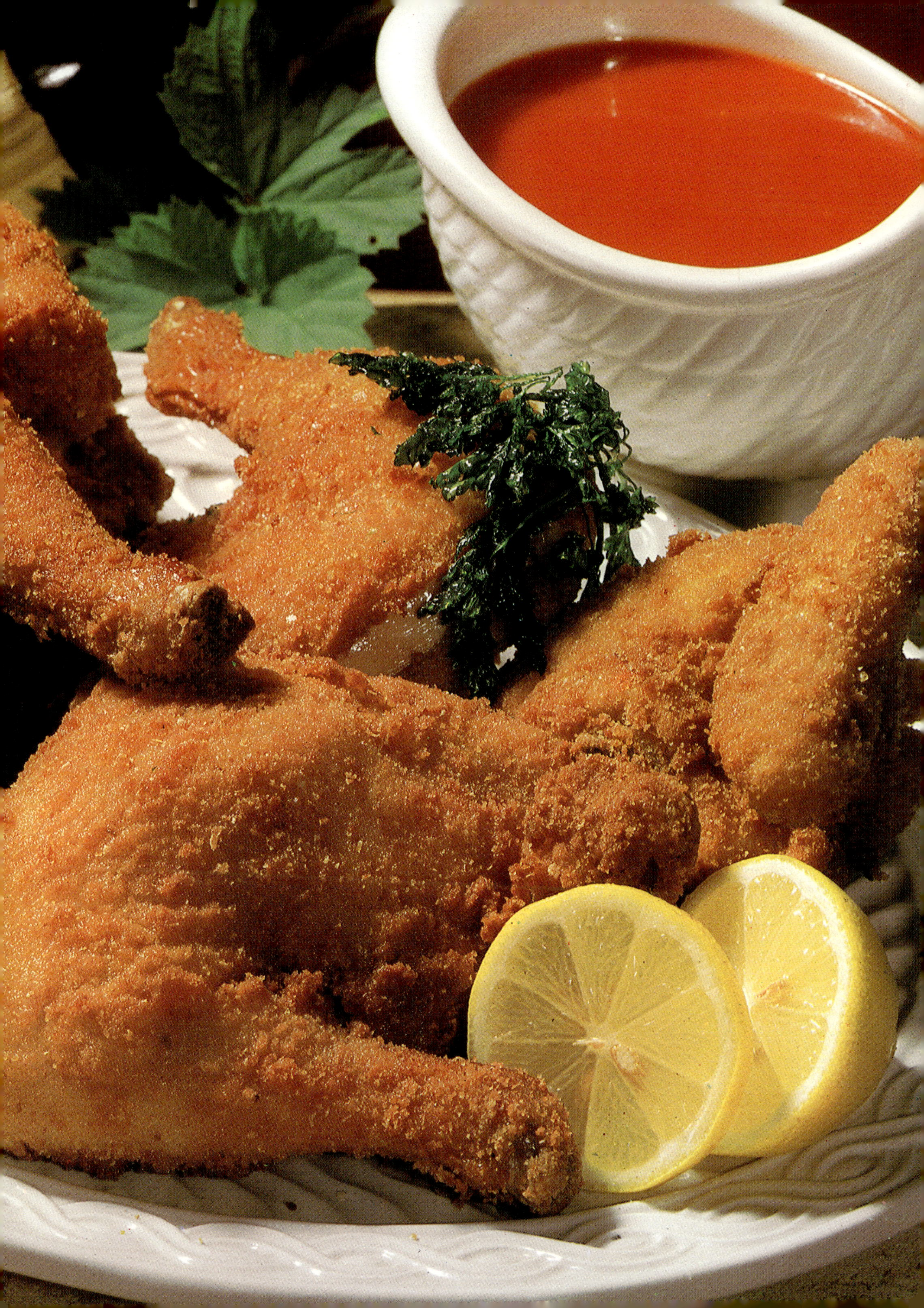

into another pan, remove the grease by laying sheets of absorbent paper on it, then add the egg yolk and reheat, stirring, without boiling. Garnish the duck with sprigs of cress. Serve with baked tomatoes, macaroni and the sauce handed separately.

Beef Tongue in Piquant Sauce

SERVES 6

3 lb pickled beef tongue
2 oz bacon, cut into strips
6 anchovy fillets, soaked, drained and cut into strips
4 tablespoons olive oil
2 tbs butter
1 carrot, diced
1 clove garlic, minced
salt, pepper
1 tablespoon chopped parsley
1 teaspoon dried basil
1 cup dry white wine
½ cup water
1 pickled gherkin, diced
¾ oz capers, roughly chopped
1 tablespoon cornstarch
½ cup sour cream
2 tomatoes, quartered
6 sprigs parsley

Soak the beef tongue in water for 1 hour. Drain. Cook in boiling water for 1 hour. Drain, remove the skin and gristle. Make incisions in the tongue and insert the strips of bacon and anchovy. Heat the oil and butter in a pan, add the carrot, garlic crushed with salt, parsley and basil and fry for 5 minutes, stirring. Put the tongue in the pan and brown on all sides for 5 minutes. Pour in the wine and water, add seasoning, cover and stew for 2 hours.

Remove the tongue from the pan and keep hot on a dish. Sieve the remaining contents of the pan and return to the pan. Add the gherkin and capers. Mix the cornstarch with a little water and add to the sauce. Bring to the boil, remove from the heat and stir in the sour cream. Do not reboil the sauce. Cut the tongue into slices ½ inch thick and arrange on a dish. Pour some of the sauce over and serve the rest separately. Garnish with tomato quarters and sprigs of parsley.

Duck marinated in red wine

Duck Marinated in Red Wine

2 cups red wine
1 large onion, chopped
1 clove garlic, minced
2 anchovy fillets, soaked, drained and crushed
5 green olives, chopped
½ teaspoon each dried rosemary, oregano, basil
3 lb duck, divided into eighths
salt, pepper
2 tbs butter
1 egg yolk, beaten
sprigs cress

To make the marinade, mix the wine with onion, garlic, anchovies, olives and herbs. Pour over the pieces of duck, cover and leave to marinate for 2 hours.

Remove the pieces of duck from the marinade, pat dry with absorbent paper and rub salt and pepper into them. Melt the butter in a large stewpan, fry the pieces of duck quickly for 10 minutes until golden on all sides. Pour in the marinade, cover the pan and let the duck simmer for 1 hour or until tender. If necessary, add more wine.

Transfer the pieces of duck to a hot dish. Strain the sauce

Beef tongue in piquant sauce

Milanese liver

Milanese Liver

1 lb calf's liver
4 tablespoons olive oil
1 onion, chopped
¼ lb mushrooms, sliced
¼ lb salami, cut into thin strips
½ lb tomatoes, skinned, seeded and quartered
½ cup white wine
salt, pepper, dried basil

Wash the liver and pat dry with absorbent paper. Cut into bite-sized cubes. Heat the oil in a pan, add the onion and fry for 3 minutes. Add the cubes of liver and fry on all sides for 3 minutes. Add the mushrooms, cook for a further 3 minutes, then add the salami and tomatoes. Pour over the white wine. Season with salt, pepper and basil. Cook for 3 minutes more, stirring. Transfer to a hot dish, and serve with spaghetti.

VEGETABLES AND SALADS

Florentine Asparagus

2 lb asparagus
3 tbs butter
salt, sugar
1 cup water
1 lb frozen chopped spinach
⅓ cup heavy cream
1 oz flaked almonds

Scrape the asparagus and trim off the woody ends. Melt the butter in a pan, add the asparagus and sprinkle with salt and sugar. Add the water, cover, bring to the boil and let the asparagus stew gently for 25 minutes. Drain the asparagus and keep warm. Cook the spinach according to the package instructions, mix in the cream and season with salt and sugar. Serve the asparagus with hot roast meat, garnished with the spinach mixture and flaked almonds.

Baked Celery

4 celery hearts
3 tablespoons grated Parmesan cheese
2 tbs butter

Cut the root ends off the celery. Put the celery hearts into boiling salted water and cook for 10 minutes, then drain. Grease an ovenproof dish with butter. Put in the celery, sprinkle the cheese over and dot with pieces of butter. Bake at 400° for 20 minutes.

Florentine asparagus

Venetian spinach

Venetian Spinach

2 lb spinach, washed and picked over
2 tablespoons olive oil
1½ lb tomatoes, skinned, seeded and roughly chopped
salt, pepper, dried oregano
1 oz anchovy fillets, soaked and drained
¼ cup grated Parmesan cheese
1 tbs butter

Put the spinach into a bowl, pour boiling water over it and leave for 6 minutes to blanch. Drain in a sieve. Heat the oil in a pan and stew the tomatoes for 5 minutes. Season with salt, pepper and oregano. Grease an ovenproof dish, put the spinach into it and season with salt and pepper. Put the tomatoes over the spinach, and arrange the anchovies on top. Sprinkle on Parmesan cheese and dot with flakes of butter. Bake at 425° for 10 to 15 minutes.

Baked Cauliflower

1 cauliflower, broken into florets
1¼ cups grated Parmesan cheese
4 tbs butter

Put the cauliflower into boiling salted water and cook for 5 minutes or until the stalks are only just cooked through. Drain. Grease an ovenproof dish with butter. Sprinkle in a third of the cheese. Put the cauliflower into the dish and sprinkle over the remaining cheese. Dot with half the butter divided into flakes. Bake at 425° for 10 minutes, then brown quickly under a hot grill. Brown the remaining butter in a frying pan and pour it over the cauliflower.

Stewed Fennel

1½ lb fennel bulbs
3 tbs butter
1 cup dry white wine
½ lb tomatoes, skinned and quartered
salt, pepper, paprika
sprigs parsley

Cut all withered and brown layers off the fennel bulbs. Cut off the root ends. Cut the fennel into large pieces. Melt the butter in a pan. Add the fennel and sauté for 5 minutes. Add the white wine and simmer for 5 minutes. Add the tomatoes, salt, pepper and paprika and simmer for 20 minutes longer, stirring occasionally. Adjust the seasoning and serve garnished with sprigs of parsley.

Stewed fennel

Broccoli and Ham

1½ lb broccoli, broken into florets
3 tbs butter
2 onions, finely chopped
½ cup cooked ham, diced

Put the broccoli into boiling salted water and cook for 5 to 7 minutes or until the stalks are just cooked through. Drain. Meanwhile melt the butter in a pan and sauté the onions until softened. Add the ham and fry quickly. Arrange the broccoli in a dish, with the ham mixture on top.

Stuffed Tomatoes

2 tbs butter
2 tbs flour
¾ cup hot milk
¼ cup grated Parmesan cheese
¼ lb peeled shrimp
salt, pepper
4 tomatoes, halved and seeded

Melt 1 tbs butter in a saucepan, stir in the flour and cook for 2 minutes without browning. Add the milk gradually, stirring constantly. Simmer for 2 to 3 minutes. Add the grated cheese and the prawns and season to taste. Remove from the heat and keep hot. Divide the remaining butter into knobs and place one knob in each tomato half. Place the tomatoes under the grill and cook for 3 to 4 minutes. Fill the centres with the prawn sauce, replace under the grill and leave to brown.

Stuffed Zucchini

4 large zucchini
2 tablespoons olive oil
2 onions, finely sliced
1 clove garlic, minced
salt, pepper
4 tomatoes, skinned, seeded and chopped
4 stalks celery, chopped
2 tablespoons tomato paste
½ teaspoon dried oregano
¼ cup grated Parmesan cheese

Trim the ends off the zucchini. Steam them in a little lightly salted boiling water for 5 to 8 minutes, then drain. Meanwhile heat the oil in a pan and fry the onions and the garlic minced with salt, for 3 to 4 minutes. Add all the remaining ingredients except the grated cheese. Continue cooking, stirring from time to time, until the vegetables are soft. Season to taste. Halve the zucchini and cut out the seeds. Fill the centres with the onion and tomato mixture, sprinkle with the grated cheese and brown under the grill.

Broccoli and ham

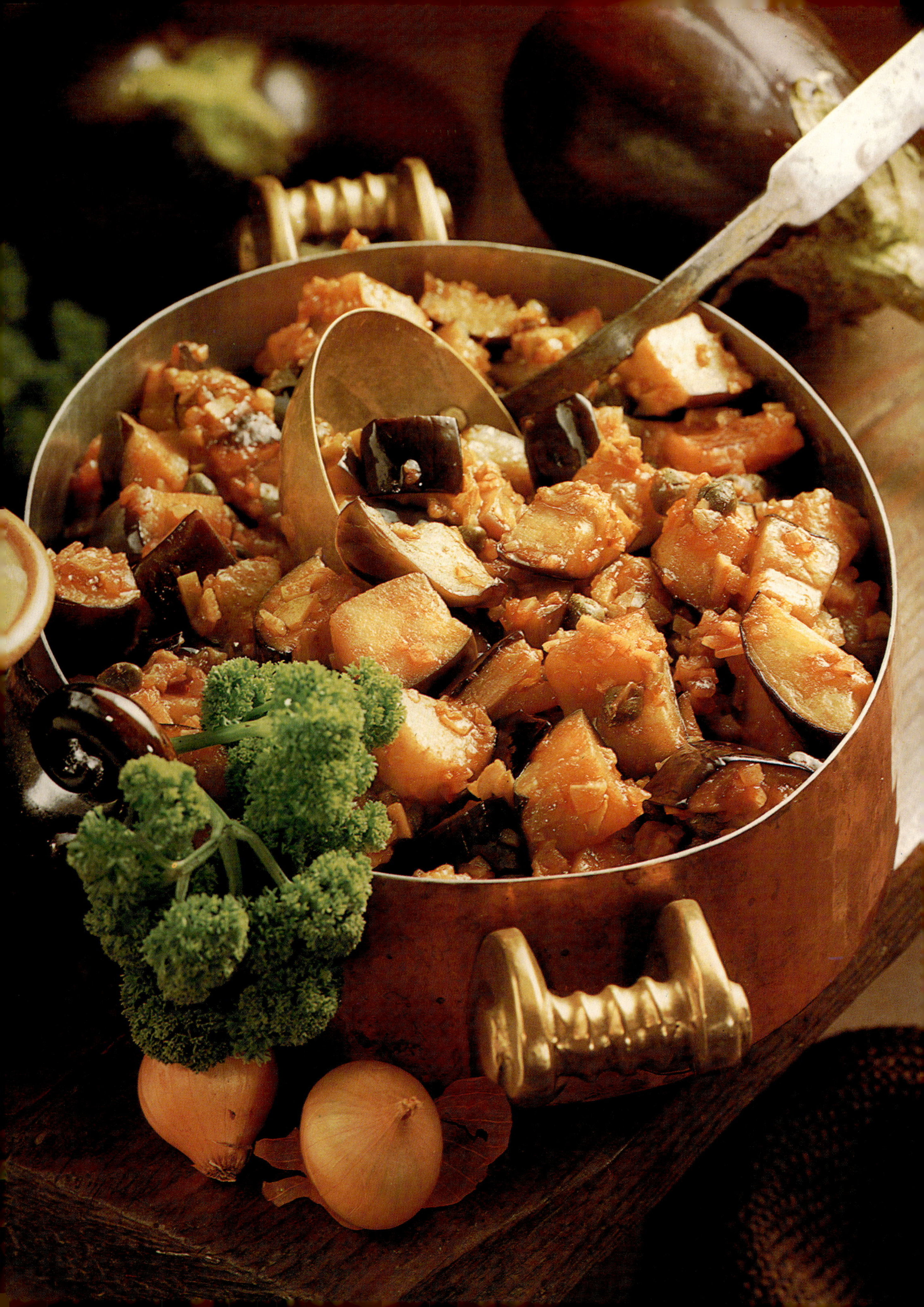

Piedmontese potato dumplings

Sicilian Eggplant

1 lb eggplant
⅓ cup olive oil
⅓ cup celery
10 stuffed olives, thinly sliced
1 tablespoon capers
salt, pepper

SAUCE
2 tablespoons olive oil
1 onion, finely chopped
3 tablespoons vinegar
1 tablespoon sugar
2 tablespoons tomato paste
1 cup stock

To make the sauce, heat the oil in a pan and fry the onion for 5 minutes until golden. Stir in the vinegar, sugar and tomato paste, add the stock and simmer for 20 minutes.

Meanwhile cut the eggplant into ½ inch cubes. Heat the olive oil in a pan and fry the eggplant for 5 minutes. Take out with a slotted spoon, drain and set aside. Trim the celery and cut into ¼ inch pieces. Fry in the oil until golden. Remove from the pan and drain. Add the eggplant celery, olives and capers to the sauce, heat until just below boiling point and season with salt and pepper.

Sicilian eggplant

Piedmontese Potato Dumplings

2 lb large potatoes
salt
1¼ cups flour
½ teaspoon grated nutmeg
4 egg yolks
⅔ cup butter
½ cup grated Parmesan cheese

Scrub the potatoes under running water and dry on absorbent paper. Sprinkle plenty of salt on a baking sheet, put the potatoes on it and bake at 425° for 45 minutes to 1 hour. Take out the potatoes and allow them to cool slightly. Skin them and put through a sieve while still warm, or mash in a large bowl with a potato masher. Make a hollow in the middle and add the flour, salt, nutmeg, egg yolks and ⅓ cup butter divided into flakes. Flour your hands and work the ingredients to a dough.

Bring water to the boil in a large pan; add salt. Form the dough into little oval shapes with 2 teaspoons. Place some of them in the water and simmer very gently for 10 minutes. The water must not be allowed to come to a full boil, or the dumplings will fall apart. Take out and drain in a sieve; add another batch to the pan. Keep the dumplings hot until all are cooked. Meanwhile melt the remaining butter. Arrange the dumplings on a hot dish, pour the melted butter over them and sprinkle with Parmesan cheese.

Parmesan eggplant

Parmesan Eggplant

1½ lb eggplant
salt, pepper
flour for coating
3 eggs, beaten
⅓ cup olive oil
½ cup grated Parmesan cheese
⅓ cup grated Emmenthal cheese
3 tbs butter

SAUCE
3 tbs butter
1 onion, diced
⅓ cup flour
6 oz canned tomato paste
2 cups stock
salt, pepper, sugar
juice ½ lemon

Slice the eggplant into rings about ½ inch thick, and salt well on both sides. Leave on a board for 30 minutes to draw out the juice.

Meanwhile make the sauce. Heat the butter in a pan, fry the onion for 5 minutes until golden. Add the flour and cook, stirring, for 2 minutes. Blend the tomato purée into the stock, gradually add to the *roux* in the pan, and simmer for 10 minutes. Season with pepper, sugar and lemon juice, and with salt if necessary.

Rinse the eggplant slices and dry with absorbent paper. Dip first in flour, then in the beaten eggs seasoned with pepper. Heat the oil in a pan until it is smoking, fry the eggplant slices for 3 minutes on each side until golden yellow. Remove from the pan and drain on absorbent paper. Mix the Parmesan and Emmenthal cheeses together.

Put half the tomato sauce in an ovenproof dish, add the eggplant in layers, sprinkling plenty of cheese over each layer. Finish with the rest of the tomato sauce and a final sprinkling of cheese. Dot the top of the casserole with flakes of butter. Cover and bake at 400° for 30 minutes.

Roman Peppers

4 tbs butter
1 lb onions, finely chopped
1 clove garlic, minced
salt, pepper
1 lb green peppers, seeded and cut into strips
¾ lb tomatoes, skinned and cut into quarters
1 teaspoon dried basil
1 tablespoon chopped parsley

Heat the butter in a pan and fry the onions and the garlic minced with salt, for 5 minutes until golden. Add the strips of green pepper, cover and stew over a moderate heat for 10 minutes. Add the tomatoes, basil, salt and pepper. Cover again and continue cooking for another 5 minutes. Transfer to a hot dish and sprinkle the parsley over the top.

Stuffed Peppers

2 green peppers, quartered and seeded
1 tablespoon olive oil
1 onion, finely chopped
1½ cups cooked rice
1 cup cooked chicken, diced
¼ teaspoon dried tarragon
salt, pepper
½ cup grated fontina or other soft, fat cheese

Blanch the green peppers in lightly salted boiling water for 5 to 8 minutes. Drain and keep hot. Heat the oil in a pan and fry the onion until it is lightly browned. Add the rice, chicken, tarragon and seasoning. Heat through, then pile the mixture into the green pepper quarters. Top with the grated cheese and place under the grill to brown.

Stuffed eggplant

Stuffed Eggplant

1½ lb eggplant
salt
4 tbs butter
1 onion, chopped
¼ lb provolone or other crumbly cheese
2 hard-cooked eggs, chopped
1 oz anchovy fillets, soaked and drained
1 tablespoon capers
1 tablespoon chopped parsley
1 teaspoon chopped dill
½ lb tomatoes, skinned and sliced
¼ cup grated Parmesan cheese

Halve the eggplant lengthwise and sprinkle salt over the cut surfaces. Put into a large shallow pan of cold water, cut side upwards, cover and bring to the boil. Simmer for 5 minutes. Remove from the pan and drain. Scoop out the flesh to within ¼ inch of the sides, and chop it.

To make the stuffing, melt 2 tbs butter in a pan and fry the onion gently until it begins to soften. Add the chopped eggplant and stew for another 5 minutes. Crumble the cheese and add to the pan with the hard-cooked eggs, anchovies, capers, parsley and dill. Mix well.

Grease a large ovenproof dish and put the tomato slices in it. Fill the eggplant halves with the stuffing and arrange side by side on the tomatoes. Sprinkle with Parmesan cheese and dot with the remaining butter, divided into flakes. Cover and bake at 425° for 45 minutes. Take the lid off the dish 10 minutes before the end of cooking time so that a brown crust forms on top.

Fried potatoes with hazelnuts

Florentine Potatoes

1 lb spinach, washed and picked over
3 anchovy fillets, soaked, drained and chopped
⅓ cup grated Gouda cheese
salt, pepper, grated nutmeg
2 lb potatoes, boiled in their skins, skinned and sliced
1 cup sour cream

Cook the spinach until tender, in no other water except that which clings to the leaves. Drain and chop. Mix the anchovy fillets and grated cheese with the spinach. Season with salt, pepper and grated nutmeg.

Grease an ovenproof dish with butter and put the spinach mixture into the dish. Place the potatoes on top. Season again with salt. Beat up the sour cream and pour it over the potatoes. Bake at 400° for 20 minutes.

Fried Potatoes with Hazelnuts

3 lb potatoes
oil for deep frying
salt
1 cup hazelnuts, finely chopped

Peel the potatoes and using a melon scoop or teaspoon, scoop out ¾ inch balls. Pat dry with absorbent paper. Heat the oil to 400°, immerse the potato balls briefly in the oil to seal the outside. Take out and allow to cool for 10 minutes. Meanwhile, reduce the temperature of the oil to 325°.

Return the potatoes to the pan and fry for another 10 minutes, until brown. Remove from the oil and drain. Season the hazelnuts well with salt and toss the potato balls in this mixture. Serve hot.

Omelettes with Vegetable Filling

8 eggs
5 tablespoons milk
⅓ cup grated Parmesan cheese
salt, pepper
½ teaspoon each dried basil, oregano
4 tablespoons olive oil

FILLING
3 tablespoons olive oil
2 onions, finely chopped
2 cloves garlic, minced
½ lb frozen spinach, thawed
5 oz celeriac, grated
1 tablespoon chopped parsley
salt, pepper

To make the filling, heat the oil in a pan and gently sauté the onions and garlic for 5 minutes. Add the spinach, celeriac and parsley. Season with salt and pepper, cover and stew for another 10 minutes.

Meanwhile beat the eggs, milk and Parmesan cheese together for the omelettes. Season with salt, pepper and herbs. Heat 1 tablespoon oil in a frying pan for each omelette, and add a quarter of the egg mixture. Fry for 3 minutes, until the bottom of the omelette is golden yellow, place a quarter of the filling on top of the omelette and fold in half. Take out of the pan and keep hot until all the omelettes are cooked.

Milanese vegetable casserole

Milanese Vegetable Casserole

1 cup bacon, diced
3 small onions, quartered
½ lb kohlrabi or turnips, diced
½ lb carrots, sliced
2 leeks, sliced
2 red peppers, seeded and cut into strips
1 lb peas
1 cup stock
salt, pepper, sugar, Tabasco sauce

Fry the bacon in a pan until the fat runs. Add the onions and cook them in the bacon fat for 5 minutes, stirring. Add the other vegetables and the stock. Season with salt and pepper, cover and simmer over a gentle heat for 30 minutes. Adjust the seasoning with salt, pepper, sugar and Tabasco sauce.

Sicilian vegetable casserole

Sicilian Vegetable Casserole

5 tablespoons olive oil
1 lb eggplant, peeled and diced
¾ lb tomatoes, skinned, seeded and coarsely chopped
1 lb green and red peppers, seeded and cut into strips
2 onions, sliced
1 clove garlic, minced
salt, cayenne, paprika
¼ lb black olives, pitted and sliced
¼ lb green olives, pitted and sliced
3 tablespoons chopped parsley

Heat the oil in a stewpan and add all the vegetables, including garlic. Sauté for 5 minutes, shaking the pan so that the vegetables do not stick. Season with salt, cayenne and paprika. Cover the pan and let the vegetables cook in their own juices for 20 minutes. Add a little water during cooking if necessary. Add the olives and cook for another 10 minutes. Sprinkle parsley over the stew before serving.

Rivoli salad

Rivoli Salad

2 tbs butter
2 boneless chiken breasts
¾ lb frozen shrimp, thawed
2 celery hearts, thinly sliced
1 small honeydew melon

DRESSING
4 tablespoons mayonaise
2 tablespoons heavy cream
1 teaspoon Tabasco sauce

Melt the butter in a frying pan and fry the chicken breasts on both sides, about 10 minutes. Take them out of the pan and allow to cool. Cut into thin strips and place in a bowl.

Reserve 8 shrimps for the garnish. Add the rest to the pieces of chicken. Add the celery, and mix well together.

Cut a lid off the melon, remove the seeds with a tablespoon and scoop out balls of the melon flesh with a melon scoop. Add them to the salad. Remove the scraps of melon left inside the skin of the fruit, and fill the melon with the salad. Mix the mayonnaise with the cream and Tabasco sauce and pour over the salad. Garnish with the reserved shrimps and serve.

Genoese Salad

¾ lb red snapper fillets
juice 1 lemon
1 cup water
5 oz canned octopus
¼ lb frozen shrimp, thawed
2 onions, thinly sliced
1 small pickled cucumber, thinly sliced
2 tomatoes, skinned, seeded and quartered
¼ lb canned French beans

DRESSING
⅓ cup olive oil
2 tablespoons wine vinegar
1 teaspoon prpared mustard
salt, pepper

Poach the red snapper fillets in the lemon juice and water for 10 minutes. Drain and flake. Cut the octopus into bite-sized pieces. Put the snapper, octopus and shrimp in a bowl. Add the onions, pickled cucumber, tomatoes and French beans, and mix carefully. Mix the dressing ingredients together and pour over the salad. Allow to stand for 20 minutes before serving, to allow the flavors to mingle.

Tuna and Egg Salad (see page 29)

½ clove garlic
½ lettuce
4 tomatoes, skinned and quartered
1 red pepper, seeded and cut into strips
1 cucumber, thinly sliced
2 small onions, thinly sliced
5 oz canned tuna, broken into chunks
8 black olives
2 hard-cooked eggs, cut into eighths

DRESSING
⅓ cup olive oil
2 tablespoons wine vinegar
1 teaspoon prepared mustard
salt, pepper

Rub a salad bowl with the cut side of the garlic clove. Line the bowl with lettuce leaves. Arrange the remaining salad ingredients on top. Mix the dressing ingredients together and pour over the salad.

Genoese salad

Artichoke Salad

6 artichokes
3 tomatoes, sliced
1 green pepper, seeded and diced
1 tablespoon chopped parsley

DRESSING
$\frac{1}{3}$ cup olive oil
2 tablespoons wine vinegar
1 clove garlic, minced
salt, pepper, sugar

Cut off the tips of the artichoke leaves and boil the artichokes for 35 minutes in well salted water. Drain. Pull the leaves apart and cut off the lower, edible parts. Cut the artichoke hearts into narrow strips. Mix the artichokes, tomatoes and green pepper.

To make the dressing, mix the olive oil with the vinegar, garlic minced with salt, pepper and sugar. Pour over the salad and mix well. Allow to stand for 20 minutes, sprinkle with chopped parsley and serve.

Sicilian Salad

1 green pepper, seeded and cut into strips
1 red pepper, seeded and cut into strips
3 apples, peeled, cored and thinly sliced
4 tomatoes, cut into eighths
1 onion, finely chopped

DRESSING
$\frac{1}{3}$ cup olive oil
2 tablespoons wine vinegar
1 teaspoon prepared mustard
salt, pepper, suga

Mix all the salad ingredients in a bowl. To make the dressing, mix together the olive oil, vinegar and mustard, and season with salt, pepper and a pinch of sugar. Pour the dressing over the salad, mix, cover and refrigerate for 15 minutes.

Artichoke salad

SAUCES

Green Sauce

1 small onion, finely chopped
1 clove garlic, minced
salt, pepper
2 anchovy fillets, soaked, drained and mashed
1 tablespoon capers
2 tablespoons chopped parsley
2 hard-cooked eggs (optional) mashed
4 tablespoons olive oil
juice $\frac{1}{2}$ lemon

Put the onion, garlic minced with salt, anchovy fillets, capers and parsley into a bowl. Add the hard-cooked eggs, if used, and the olive oil and lemon juice. Stir well, season highly with salt and pepper, cover and refrigerate for 30 minutes before serving. For a more traditional version, the hard-cooked eggs should be omitted. Serve with hot or cold meat and poultry.

Solferino Sauce

$1\frac{1}{2}$ cups tomato juice
4 tbs butter
2 tablespoons chopped parsley
1 tablespoon chopped dill
4 tablespoons chopped cress
$\frac{1}{4}$ teaspoon dried tarragon
1 shallot or small onion, grated
1 tablespoon lemon juice
salt, cayenne

Put the tomato juice in a pan and cook uncovered over a moderate heat for about 25 minutes, until it has reduced to a syrupy consistency. Cream the butter in a bowl and mix in the chopped fresh herbs, dried tarragon, grated shallot or onion and the lemon juice. Add the herb butter to the reduced tomato juice, beat the sauce well with a wire whisk and season to taste with salt and cayenne pepper. Serve with grilled or fried meat.

Roman Sauce

3 tbs butter
4 tbs flour
$1\frac{1}{2}$ cups stock
1 tablespoon sugar
3 tablespoons wine vinegar
3 tablespoons raisins, chopped
3 tablespoons pine nuts, chopped
1 tablespoon chopped parsley
salt, pepper

Melt the butter in a pan. Add the flour and cook for 3 minutes, stirring, until you have a lightly browned *roux*. Pour in the stock gradually, stirring. Simmer over a gentle heat for 10 minutes, stirring from time to time.

Melt the sugar in a thick pan and allow to brown. Pour in the vinegar. Add the brown sauce, the raisins, the pine nuts and parsley, and season to taste with salt and pepper. Serve with roast meat.

Green sauce

Green Pepper Sauce

2 tablespoons olive oil
1 cup bacon, finely diced
1 onion, finely chopped
1 clove garlic, minced
2 green peppers, seeded and diced
4 tomatoes, skinned, seeded and chopped
salt, pepper
$\frac{1}{3}$ cup grated Parmesan cheese

Heat the olive oil in a pan and fry the bacon for 2 minutes. Add the onion and garlic and fry until softened. Add the peppers and tomatoes, cover and stew over a moderate heat for 25 minutes. Season to taste with salt and pepper and stir in the cheese. Serve with pasta, fish or meat.

Mushroom Sauce

2 tablespoons olive oil
$\frac{1}{2}$ cup bacon, finely diced
$\frac{1}{2}$ onion, finely chopped
1 small clove garlic, minced
1 teaspoon flour
$\frac{1}{2}$ cup dry white wine
1 teaspoon lemon juice
1 tablespoon chopped parsley
$\frac{1}{2}$ teaspoon dried basil
salt, pepper
$\frac{1}{4}$ lb mushrooms, chopped

Heat the olive oil in a pan and fry the bacon for 2 minutes, then add the onion and garlic and fry until softened. Add the flour and cook for 2 minutes, stirring. Pour in the wine and add the lemon juice, herbs, seasoning and mushrooms. Simmer for 10 minutes. Serve with poultry and veal.

Liver Sauce

$\frac{3}{4}$ lb calf's liver
4 tablespoons olive oil
1 cup bacon, finely diced
2 onions, chopped
2 teaspoons flour
1 cup stock
2 tablespoons tomato paste
$\frac{1}{2}$ bay leaf
1 clove garlic, minced
salt, pepper
$\frac{1}{2}$ teaspoon dried oregano
1 tablespoon chopped parsley

Cut the liver into pieces and purée in an electric blender, or put through a food processor, using the finest blade. Heat the oil in a pan and fry the bacon and onions until golden. Add the flour and cook for 2 minutes, stirring. Pour in the stock gradually, stirring constantly. Simmer for 5 minutes.

Add the tomato purée, liver, bay leaf and garlic. Season with salt, pepper and oregano. Simmer for another 5 minutes, then add the chopped parsley. Serve with pasta or rice.

DESSERTS, CAKES AND PASTRIES

Neapolitan Cheesecake

2 cups flour
1 egg yolk
1 cup sugar
salt
1 cup butter, chilled
1 egg white, lightly beaten
confectioners sugar
FILLING
¼ cup pearl barley, soaked overnight and drained
2 cups milk
¾ lb cream cheese
2 egg yolks
1 cup fine sugar
2 cups candied fruits, coarsely chopped
grated rind 1 lemon
cinnamon
2 tablespoons orange-flower water or 1 tablespoon orange liqueur

Put the pearl barley and milk into a pan, bring to the boil, cover and simmer gently until the pearl barley has absorbed all the milk, about 20 minutes. Allow to cool slightly. Meanwhile put the cream cheese into a bowl with the egg yolks and sugar, and beat until smooth. Mix in the chopped candied fruits, grated lemon rind, a pinch of cinnamon and the orange-flower water or orange liqueur. Finally mix in the pearl barley. Cover and let stand for 1 hour.

To make the pastry, put the flour on a board, make a hollow in the centre, add the egg yolk and sprinkle with the sugar and a pinch of salt. Put the butter in flakes around the edge. Using a knife, chop all together, working from the outside inwards. Knead quickly with cool hands to a smooth dough. Cover and refrigerate for 30 minutes.

Roll out two-thirds of the pastry into a circle 11 inches across. Roll out the remaining pastry into a circle 9½ inches across. Put the larger circle into a 9½ inch baking pan, pressing up the edges. Place the filling on this base, smooth the surface, and cover with the second circle of pastry, pressing the pastry edges well together. Brush the top with beaten egg white. Bake at 350° for 1 hour.

Take the pan out of the oven, turn out the cheesecake, put on a dish and allow to cool. Dust with sifted confectioners sugar.

Rice Cheesecake

2 cups flour
1 egg
½ cup fine sugar
salt
½ cup butter, chilled
FILLING
¼ cup pudding rice
1 cup milk
1 lb cream cheese
1 cup fine sugar
2 teaspoons vanilla sugar
¼ cup butter
2 eggs, separated
1 tablespoon cornstarch
salt
1 cup currants, soaked and drained
2 tbs breadcrumbs

To make the pastry, put the flour on a board, make a hollow in the centre and break the egg into it. Sprinkle with the sugar and a pinch of salt. Put the butter in flakes around the edge. Working from the outside inwards, knead fast to make a smooth dough. Cover and refrigerate for 30 minutes.

To make the filling, put the rice in a pan with the milk and bring to the boil. Leave over a very low heat for 15 minutes, to allow the rice to swell. Cool slightly. Put the cream cheese into a bowl with the sugar, vanilla sugar, butter, egg yolks, cornstarch and a pinch of salt. Beat until smooth. Mix in the rice and the currants. Beat the egg whites until stiff and fold into the cheese mixture.

Roll out the pastry to a circle ¼ inch thick. Line a 10 inch baking pan with the pastry, pressing up the sides to a depth of 1½ inches. Sprinkle the pastry with the breadcrumbs. Spread the filling over the pastry shell and smooth the surface with a wet knife. Bake on the bottom shelf of the oven at 400° for 1 hour 10 minutes. Turn the heat off and leave the cheesecake to cool in the oven before turning it out of the pan.

Neapolitan gâteau

Neapolitan Gâteau

¾ cup butter
1½ cups fine sugar
2 eggs
1½ cups ground almonds
grated rind 1 lemon
4 cups flour

FILLING
½ cup each apricot, cherry, raspberry, blackcurrant jelly

FROSTING AND DECORATION
2 cups confectioners sugar
2 tablespoons hot water
2 tablespoons maraschino liqueur
½ cup heavy cream
12 cocktail cherries

Beat the butter, sugar and eggs in a bowl until light and foamy. Add the almonds and lemon rind. Sprinkle in the flour and first stir, then knead, to make a smooth dough. Cover and refrigerate for 1 hour.

Divide the pastry into five. Roll out each portion on a floured surface to ⅛ inch thick. Using the closed ring of a 9½ inch spring clip baking pan, cut out circles to fit the pan. Put one circle on the greased base of the pan and spread with apricot jelly, add the other circles, spreading in turn with cherry, raspberry and blackcurrant jelly, and covering the last layer of jelly with the fifth pastry circle. Put the ring around the circles of pastry and close it. Bake on the bottom shelf of the oven at 400° for 45 minutes.

Take the pan out of the oven, allow to cool, turn out the gâteau and put it on a plate. To make the frosting, mix the confectioners sugar with the hot water and add the liqueur. Stir until the frosting is smooth and shiny. Use to cover the top and sides of the gâteau. Just before the frosting hardens, mark out 12 portions on the surface with the back of a knife. Whip the cream until stiff, put into a pastry bag and pipe a rosette on each portion. Top each rosette with a cherry.

Milanese gâteau

Milanese Gâteau

½ cup butter
6 eggs
2 cups fine sugar
salt
1½ cups flour
1½ cups raspberry liqueur (or other fruit liqueur)
½ cup raspberry juice (or other fruit juice)

FILLING
 5 oz marzipan
¾ cup raspberry jelly

TOP
½ cup apricot jelly, melted
¼ lb marzipan
½ cup raspberry jelly

SIDES
¼ cup apricot jelly
1 teaspoon water
5 oz marzipan
3 oz small macaroons

Melt the butter and cool slightly. Beat the eggs, sugar and a pinch of salt in a bowl over hot water until you have a light, creamy mixture which will hold a peak. Do not let the water boil. Take the mixture off the heat and continue beating until it is cool. Fold the flour in lightly, then stir in the melted and nearly cool butter. Line a spring-clip 11 inch baking pan with greased wax paper. Dust with flour, fill with the cake mixture and smooth the top. Bake at 350° for 50 minutes. Turn out on to a wire rack and leave to cool.

Slice the cake into two layers. Mix the fruit liqueur and juice and pour over both layers. Leave to soak.

To make the filling, roll out the marzipan on wax paper to a circle 25 cm/10 inches across. Spread raspberry jelly over one half of the cake. Cover with the marzipan and place the other half on top.

To decorate the top of the cake, brush with melted apricot jelly. Roll out the marzipan on wax paper and cut out 12 circles, each 2 inches across. Put a teaspoon of raspberry jelly in the center of each circle and place in a ring round the cake.

To decorate the sides, heat the apricot jelly and water, stirring until smooth. Brush the sides of the cake with this glaze, keeping back 2 teaspoons. Roll out the marzipan to make two strips each 1½ inches wide and 16 inches long. Stick these to the glazed sides of the cake. Use the reserved apricot glaze to stick the macaroons to the sides of the cake.

Chill the gâteau before serving.

Piedmontese Cakes

2 cups milk
½ cup sugar
1 cup semolina
¾ cup butter
salt
½ lb preserved morello cherries, chopped
1 egg
½ cup kirsch

COATING
1 egg yolk
2 tablespoons milk
⅓ cup breadcrumbs
confectioners sugar

Put the milk, sugar, semolina, 2 tbs butter and a pinch of salt into a pan. Bring to the boil, stirring. Simmer for 10 minutes, stirring, until the mixture is quite thick. Mix the cherries with the egg and kirsch, then stir into the pan. Grease a cookie sheet and spread the semolina mixture on it about ¾ inch thick. Mark into 1½ inch squares. Leave to cool for 30 minutes.

Beat the egg yolk and milk together. Cut the semolina mixture into squares along the marked lines. Dip the squares into the egg and milk and then into the breadcrumbs. Melt the remaining butter in a frying pan and fry the cakes for 3 minutes on each side, until golden brown. Dust with icing sugar. Serve hot, or leave on a wire rack to cool.

Sicilian Cannelloni

2 tbs butter
2 cups flour
2 tbs sugar
1 egg
salt
about ½ cup white wine
1 egg white
oil for deep frying

FILLING
1 lb cream cheese
¼ lb confectioners sugar
2 teaspoons vanilla sugar
¼ lb candied fruits, finely chopped
2 oz chocolate, finely chopped

Melt the butter and allow it to cool. Put the flour in a bowl and make a hollow in the middle. Place the sugar, butter, egg and a pinch of salt in the hollow. Working from the outside inwards, knead to a smooth dough. Make another hollow in the dough and work in the white wine gradually. The dough must not be too stiff or too slack. Cover and refrigerate for 1 hour.

Meanwhile, prepare the filling. Beat the cream cheese, confectioners sugar and vanilla sugar until smooth. Mix in the chopped candied fruits and chocolate. Cover and refrigerate for 20 minutes.

Roll out the dough on a floured surface to ⅛ inch thick. Using a notched wheel-type cookie cutter if you have one, cut out 4½ inch squares. Make smooth rolls of foil 6 inches long, one for each pastry square. Roll each square of pastry diagonally around the foil. Brush the outer corner with egg white and press lightly on to the pastry to seal the roll.

Sicilian cannelloni

Heat the oil and fry the rolls for 3 minutes until golden brown. Turn them in the hot oil several times during cooking, using a slotted spoon, so that they color on all sides. Remove from the pan with a slotted spoon, drain well on absorbent paper and allow to cool. Carefully remove the foil from inside the rolls when they have cooled. Finish cooling the rolls for another 15 minutes on a wire rack. Using a teaspoon, fill the rolls with the cheese mixture.

Florentines

Florentines

1½ cups chopped almonds
½ cup candied lemon peel, finely chopped
½ cup candied orange peel, finely chopped
¼ cup candied cherries, finely chopped
1 tbs crystallised ginger, finely chopped
¾ cup sugar
2 teaspoons vanilla sugar
1 cup flour
grated rind 1 lemon
3 tbs butter
½ cup milk
½ cup cream
salt
¼ lb semi-sweet chocolate

Mix the chopped almonds with the candied lemon and orange peel, cherries, ginger, sugar, vanilla sugar, flour and grated lemon rind. Heat the butter with the milk, cream and salt in a large pan. Stir in the almond mixture. Simmer gently, stirring, for 5 minutes.

Line a cookie sheet with greased foil. Using a teaspoon dipped in cold water, place little mounds of the almond mixture wide apart on the foil. (Florentines run into each other while cooking if not widely spaced). Smooth flat with a wet knife. Bake at 350° for 25 minutes.

Remove the cookies from the foil as soon as you take them out of the oven, working very carefully, because they are extremely fragile. Melt the chocolate in a bowl standing over hot water; dip the underside of each cookie into it, place on a wire rack with the chocolate-coated side upwards and draw on wavy lines with a fork. Leave to cool and let the chocolate dry. Larger florentines may also be made, to be broken into pieces for serving.

Panettone

Paganini

1¼ lb frozen puff pastry, thawed
2 egg yolks, beaten

FILLING
4 egg whites
2 cups confectioners sugar
2 teaspoons vanilla sugar
3 cups ground almonds
½ teaspoon ground cinnamon
salt

FROSTING
2 cups confectioners sugar
3 tablespoons water
2 tablespoons rosewater

Roll out the pastry on a floured surface to ⅛ inch thick, and cut into strips 3 inches wide and 6 inches long. To make the filling, beat the egg whites in a bowl until stiff. Gradually add the sifted confectioners sugar, the vanilla sugar, ground almonds, cinnamon and a pinch of salt. Spread this filling on the pastry strips and roll them up. Glaze with beaten egg yolk. Brush a cookie sheet with cold water and place the pastry rolls on it. Bake at 425° for 25 minutes. Cool the pastries on a wire rack.

To make the frosting, sift the confectioners sugar and mix with the water and rosewater. Paint over the pastries and allow to dry.

Milanese Cookies

3 cups flour
2 eggs
grated rind 1 lemon
salt
1 cup fine sugar
2½ cups ground almonds
1 cup butter
2 egg yolks, beaten
½ cup chopped almonds

Put the flour on a board and make a hollow in the centre. Break in the eggs, add the grated lemon rind and a pinch of salt. Sprinkle the sugar and ground almonds over them. Divide the butter into flakes and place round the outside of the flour. Working from the outside inwards, knead to a smooth dough. Cover and refrigerate for 30 minutes.

Roll out the dough to ⅛ inch thick. Cut out round biscuits 2½ inches across. Brush the biscuits with beaten egg yolk and scatter chopped almonds over them. Place the biscuits on a greased cookie sheet and bake at 400° for 15 minutes. Remove from the cookie sheet and cool on a wire rack.

Mandolini

3 egg whites
¾ cup fine sugar
¾ cup ground almonds
¾ cup flour

Beat the egg whites until stiff, gradually adding the sugar. Fold in the ground almonds and flour. Divide the mixture into little balls the size of a walnut, and shape them into sticks the length of a finger on a floured surface. Grease a baking sheet, place the biscuits on it about 1 inch apart, and bake at 350° for 17 minutes. Cool the biscuits on a wire rack.

Panettone

1½ oz fresh yeast or ¾ oz dried
  yeast
½ cup sugar
about ⅔ cup lukewarm milk
4 cups flour
½ teaspoon salt
6 eggs
1 cup butter
¾ cup candied lemon peel,
  chopped
¾ cup candied orange peel,
  chopped
¾ cup candied cherries, chopped
2 cups raisins
1 tablespoon flour

To make the dough, cream the fresh yeast with 1 teaspoon sugar and a little of the milk, then add the remaining milk. (If using dried yeast, dissolve 1 teaspoon sugar in the milk, sprinkle on the yeast and stir well.) Leave to stand in a warm place for about 10 minutes. Meanwhile sift the flour and salt into a bowl. Make a hollow in the centre and pour in the yeast mixture. Add the remaining sugar and the eggs. Divide ¾ cup butter into flakes and place on top. Working from the outside inwards, knead to a soft dough.

In another bowl, mix the chopped candied peel and chopped candied cherries with the raisins and 1 tablespoon flour. Knead into the dough. Grease a 7 inch baking pan, put the dough into it, cover and leave to rise for 20 minutes. Bake on the bottom shelf of the oven at 425° for 1 hour. Melt the remaining butter and half way through the baking time brush this over the top of the cake.

Take the cake out of the oven and turn out on to a wire rack to cool. Keep for 24 hours before eating.

INDEX

Almonds:
    Mandolini 79
    Milanese cookies 79
    Paganini 79
Anchovies:
    Anchovy pizza 26
    Pizza Dalida 30
    Pizza Giugliano 27
    Sicilian anchovies 35
    Spaghetti alla Caprese 15
Antipasti 7
Artichokes:
    Antipasti 7
    Artichoke salad 68
Asparagus:
    Antipasti 7
    Florentine asparagus 56

Beef:
    Braised beef with rosemary 47
    Lasagne 20
    Macaroni alla Fiorentina 18
    Macaroni alla Siciliana 18
    Meatballs in tomato sauce 48
    Neapolitan beef soup 11
    Ravioli alla Piemontese 21
    Sirlion steak in wine sauce 48
    Spaghetti alla Bolognese 17
    Beef tongue in piquant sauce 54
Broccoli and ham 59

Calzoni 8
Cauliflower: Baked cauliflower 57
Celery: Baked celery 56
Cheese:
    Fonduta 9
    Macaroni Amatrice 17
    Neapolitan cheesecake 73
    Parmesan Eggplant 62
    Rice cheesecake 73
    Risotto alla Milanese 23
    Salami Bolognese-style 9
    Sicilian cannelloni 76
    see also Mozzarella; Ricotta
Chicken:
    Deep-fried chicken 52
    Florentine chicken 51
    Rivoli salad 66
Cod: Florentine baked fish 35

Duck marinated in red wine 54
Dumplings:
    Backed gnocchi 22
    Piedmontese potato dumplings 61
Eel:
    Baked eel 32
    Seafood patties 35
Eggplant:
    Macaroni alla Siciliana 18
    Parmesan eggplant 62
    Sicilian eggplant 61
    Sicilian vegetable casserole 65
    Stuffed eggplant
Eggs: Tuna and egg salad 67

Fennel: Stewed fennel 58
Fish:
    Antipasti 7
    Fish soup 13
    Spaghetti alla Marinara 15
    see also Cod; Halibut; Mackerel; Octopus; Sole; Trout; Tuna
Florentines 77
Fonduta 9

Gnocchi: Baked gnocchi 22
Green sauce 71

Halibut: Ligurian fish casserole 34
Ham:
    Broccoli and ham 59
    Calzoni 8
    Pizza Giugliano 27
    Roman soup 12
    Sicilian veal roll 38
Hazelnuts: Fried potatoes with hazelnuts 64

Lamb:
    Roman lamb cutlets 48
    Spicy lamb cutlets 49
Lasagne 20
Liver:
    Liver sauce 72
    Milanese liver 55

Macaroni:
    Macaroni alla Fiorentina 18
    Macaroni alla Siciliana 18
    Macaroni Amatrice 17
Mackerel:
    Fish soup 13
    Stuffed mackerel 32
Mandolini 79
Marsala: Veal and pork scallops in Marsala sauce 46
Meatballs in tomato sauce 48
Melon:
    Antipasti 7
    Rivoli salad 66
Milanese cookies 79
Milanese gâteau 75
Milanese liver 55
Milanese roast veal 39
Milanese turkey 52
Mileanese veal scallops 46
Milanese vegetable casserole 65
Minestrone: Florentine minestrone 10
Mortadella:
    Antipasti 7
    Mortadella pizza 27
Mozzarella:
    Calzoni 8
    Pizza alla Napoletana 31
    Pizza Giugliano 27
    Veal cutlets with mozzarella 42
Mullet: Genoese salad 67
Mushrooms:
    Mushroom sauce 72
    Risotto mould 23
    Trout with mushrooms 37
Mussels:
    Baked mussels 36
    Seafood patties 35
    Spaghetti alla Marinara 15

Neapolitan beef soup 11
Neapolitan cheesecake 73
Neapolitan gâteau 74
Neapolitan veal stew 38
Noodles:
    Apulian noodles 19
    Noodles with herb sauce 19

Octopus: Genoese salad 67
Offal: *see* Liver *and* beef tongue
Omelettes with vegetable filling 64
Onions: Pizza Dalida 30
Osso Buco 38
Oysters: Florentine oysters 6

Paganini 79
Pancakes in broth 10
Panettone 8
Pasta: *see* individual types
Peppers:
    Green pepper sauce 72
    Roman peppers 63
    Sicilian salad 68
    Sicilian vegetable casserole 65
    Stuffed peppers 63
Piedmontese cakes 76
Pizza:
    Anchovy pizza 26
    Mortadella pizza 27
    Pizza alla Napoletana 31
    Pizza Dalida 30
    Pizza Giugliano 27
Polenta: Calabrian potenta 22
Pork:
    Lombard pork and vegetables 50
    Veal and pork scallops in Marsala sauce 46
Potatoes:
    Florentine potatoes 64
    Fried potatoes with hazelnuts 64
    Piedmontese potato dumplings 61

Ravioli alla Piemontese 21
Rice:
    Rice cheesecake 73
    Risotto alla Milanese 23
    Risotto alla Napoletana 24
    Risotto mould 23
    Vegatable risotto 24
Ricotta: Noodles with herb sauce 19
Roman sauce 71
Roman soup 12

Salads:
    Artichoke salad 68
    Genoese salad 67
    Rivoli salad 66
    Sicilian salad 68
    Tuna and egg salad 67
Salami:
    Calzoni 8
    Milanese liver 55
    Salami Bolognese-style 9
Seafood patties 35
Semolina: Baked gnocchi 22`
Shellfish: *see* individual types
Shrimp:
    Devilled shrimp 37
    Genoese salad 67
    Rivoli salad 66
    Seafood patties 35
    Stuffed tomatoes 59
Sole: Seafood patties 35
Solferino sauce 71
Spaghetti:
    Ligurian fish casserole 34
    Spaghetti alla Bolognese 17
    Spaghetti alla Caprese 15
    Spaghetti alla Carbonara 16
    Spaghetti alla Marinara 15
    Spaghetti alla Napoletana 15
Spinach:
    Florentine asparagus 56
    Florentine baked fish 35
    Florentine oysters 6
    Florentine potatoes 64
    Venetian spinach 57

Tomatoes:
    Anchovy pizza 26
    Antipasti 7
    Apulian noodles 19
    Calabrian polenta 22
    Macaroni Amatrice 17
    Meatballs in tomato sauce 48
    Pizza alla Napoletana 31
    Pizza Giugliano 27
    Risotto alla Napoletana 24
    Risotto mould 23
    Shell pasta in tomato sauce 20
    Spaghetti alla Caprese 15
    Spaghetti alla Napoletana 15
    Stuffed tomatoes 59
    Venetian spinach 57
Trout with mushrooms 37
Tuna:
    Antipasti 7
    Ligurian fish casserolé 34
    Spaghetti alla Caprese 15
    Tuna and egg salad 67
Turkey: Milanese turkey 52

Veal:
    Milanese roast veal 39
    Milanese veal scallops 46
    Neapolitan veal stew 38
    Osso Buco 38
    Piedmontese braised veal 39
    Sicilian veal roll 38
    Ticino veal scallops 43
    Veal and pork scallops in Marsala sauce 46
    Veal cutlets with mozzarella 42
    Veal scallops with herbs 42
    Veal scallops with lemon 43
Vegetables:
    Lombard pork and vegatables 50
    Milanese vegetable casserole 65
    Omelettes with vegetable filling 64
    Sicilian vegetable casserole 65
    Vegatable risotto 24

Wine:
    Duck marinated in red wine 54
    Sirloin steak in wine sauce 48

Zucchini: Stuffed zucchini 59